So You Want to be an Entrepreneur?

So You Want to be an Entrepreneur?

Jon Gillespie-Brown

CAPSTONE
be inspired!

John Wiley & Sons, Ltd

Other Wiley Editorial Offices

John Wiley & Sons Inc., 111 River Street, Hoboken, NJ 07030, USA

Jossey-Bass, 989 Market Street, San Francisco, CA 94103-1741, USA

Wiley-VCH Verlag GmbH, Boschstr. 12, D-69469 Weinheim, Germany

John Wiley & Sons Australia Ltd, 42 McDougall Street, Milton, Queensland 4064, Australia

John Wiley & Sons (Asia) Pte Ltd, 2 Clementi Loop #02-01, Jin Xing Distripark, Singapore
129809

John Wiley & Sons Canada Ltd, 22 Worcester Road, Etobicoke, Ontario, Canada M9W 1L1

CONTENTS

WHY YOU SHOULD BUY THIS BOOK

'We cannot live only for ourselves. A thousand fibres connect us with our fellow-men, and along those fibres, as sympathetic friends, our actions run as causes, and they come back to us as effects.'

Herman Melville

This book is written in an 'easy to read' style designed to help you decide if you want to become an entrepreneur, using *you* as a starting point. It's based around a series of mentor sessions, guiding you through the realities of life as an entrepreneur together with an analysis of your life, goals and ambitions. It then helps you decide if this is the life for you.

Reading it and actively taking part in each of the exercises will provide you with the best chance of succeeding as an entrepreneur, if that's the path you choose; or it will give you sufficient clarity to decide what other career options are best suited to you.

Another great reason to buy this book is because all the profits go directly to helping other would-be entrepreneurs less fortunate than you. Imagine that, just by buying this book you will contribute towards launching someone else's venture – so you will become an entrepreneur's sponsor even if you don't do it yourself.

Personally, I believe in 'giving back' and making a contribution as the universal power behind everyone's success. This could be the first lesson you learn from this book.

Start your entrepreneurial journey by <u>giving</u> and you will be more successful that you can imagine!

Who will you be supporting by buying this book?

The Grameen Foundation

'I plan to donate the proceeds from the sale of this book to an organization that I feel is making a meaningful difference, the Grameen Foundation. Grameen Foundation is a US-based nonprofit that seeks to empower the world's poorest people to lift themselves out of poverty with dignity through access to financial services and to information.

Learn more at www.grameenfoundation.org'

PREFACE

'There comes a special moment in everyone's life, a moment for which that person was born. That special opportunity, when he seizes it, will fulfil his mission – a mission for which he is uniquely qualified. In that moment, he finds greatness. It is his finest hour.'

Winston Churchill

Dear Reader,

Welcome to a book that is all about you!

Unlike many other great books in this field, this book is specifically designed to guide you through a comprehensive, personal thought process, allowing you to come to a decision about whether or not you really want to become an entrepreneur.

Being an entrepreneur is like nothing else. It is incredibly taxing yet rewarding, stressful and energizing, risky but exciting, and we are going to find out if that's the life for you.

When I got my first really serious business going at eighteen, I needed some start-up funds. With my mother's encouragement I wrote to all my wealthier relatives (the few!) trying to drum up some support. I included one of my favourite people in the world, a close family friend who owned a successfull hat factory. He wrote me a long and eloquent argument as to why <u>not</u> to start in my business and to do something else!

I was stunned, quite upset and finally indignant. I couldn't believe this successful businessman who was always cheerful and happy, the most upbeat person I have ever met, would try to crush my dreams. In hindsight I know he was just looking out for me. Despite his cheery disposition, this man had endured a long and rocky road to build his now mighty business. He wanted to save me from that . . . as it happens I wasn't to be deterred from my ambition.

While of course I want you to understand what you would be getting yourself into, I don't want to deter you from your ambition either. Whether you are 16 or 66, people will tell you that you can't or shouldn't become an entrepreneur (and for good reason, as most people fail) but don't be put off by anecdote. <u>Use this book to really test the viability of any decision.</u>

> '*The entrepreneur is our visionary, the creator in each of us. We're born with that quality and it defines our lives as we respond to what we see, hear, feel, and experience. It is developed, nurtured, and given space to flourish or is squelched, thwarted, without air or stimulation, and dies.*'
> **Michael Gerber**

Can a book really make a difference?

Don't underestimate how important something as simple as a book can be to shaping the path you will eventually take in life. Like so many other successful entrepreneurs, my own defining moment can be traced back to a book that became the impetus for me starting my first business. The book was 'How to Win Friends and Influence People', a business motivational and personal development staple nowadays, but back then I had never even heard of it or its author. I didn't even know any entrepreneurs or people that ran their own businesses.

The concept of entrepreneurship was entirely foreign to me as a career choice. My father had only ever worked for two companies in his whole life, and the expectation was that I would pursue a future in the sciences or something equally 'credible'. I certainly wasn't expected to waste my 'brains' in a business start-up. Nevertheless, this book had a profound effect on me; not only did it give me a huge amount of confidence, it also sowed the seed of a burning entrepreneurial ambition. It changed my outlook on life completely and made me realize I could do anything I put my mind to. With the help of this book, my new found confidence grew steadily until I started my first venture at the age of eighteen years. So you never know where a book is going to take you.

I have designed this book as a series of mentoring sessions, carefully thought out to make you think about, consider and plan your life based on your passions, ambitions, life phase, resources and ultimate visions – even if you don't become an entrepreneur, your life will be more focused and directed towards happiness and success after having read just the first few chapters!

Take a risk and make a life that is your 'own' without the permission of others – just like I did over twenty years ago . . .

Enjoy the book and I wish you all success in your new life.

Jon Gillespie-Brown, *www.tobeanentrepreneur.com*

ACKNOWLEDGEMENTS

'As we express our gratitude, we must never forget that the highest appreciation is not to utter words, but to live by them.'

John Fitzgerald Kennedy

Unfortunately thanking everyone that has shaped my life to this point and helped me, knowingly or not, is an impossible task. However, I will try to ensure I capture those that have helped me with this act of contribution; this book that I have produced as my ultimate thanks to those that have blessed me with their love and help over the years.

Of course, the top of my list of thanks goes to my family, especially Maria, my wife who helped with editing and working with our chosen charity.

The London Business School

To my many friends and colleagues at LBS, but especially Anne Miller, Adam Burdess, Patxi Avila-Kildal, Fredrik Samanta and John Mullins.

My many friends, entrepreneurs and mentees

Just a few that contributed directly here but I would like to thank them all in spirit.

Richard Parkes-Cordock, Adam Miller, Les Ashton, Shirin Kiral, Mark Reohorn, Greg Wood, Philip Clayden, Chantelle Ludski, Allen Barrell, Julian Costley, Dr Jan Hruska, Peter Ward, Rachel Elnaugh, Doug Richard, Richard Farleigh, Stuart Collingwood, Helen Baker, Paul Gardner and many more.

Publishers

Thanks to John Moseley for sponsoring my ideas and Jenny Ng for so ably assisting the execution of them.

Special thanks

This goes to Michael Soth who co-authored the quiz section and Nuala Mullen, my editor who transformed my ideas and words into a compelling and flowing story.

Contributors

Many others also contributed their ideas and content for the book are also thanked warmly.

So much help and work from others has gone into this charitable effort that it's hard to claim it as my own. However, I am grateful that so many are willing to help others through their own contribution.

DEDICATION

This book is dedicated to my family.

My entrepreneurial passion started at a very young age and I have to thank my parents for not quashing my ambitions before they got going. I am sure they thought I was crazy on more than one occasion but they always inspired, helped, funded or encouraged me.

I got my curiosity and inventiveness from my father, who I remember as always tinkering with things. Indeed, he came up with quite a few of his own ideas, such as a special insurance package for householders to record their belongings, and a portable saddle back for pushbikes. These never got past the 'prototype' stage, unfortunately.

From my mother (and grandmother) I got the energy, passion and determination to succeed.

I am not sure to whom should go the credit for my stubbornness, persistence and will to win, nor my need for 'fair play', compassion or justice. But they have helped a great deal in my entrepreneurial journey to date.

For my wife and boys; they are my shining light – my beacon when I am 'lost at sea'; my solid ground when I feel cast adrift . . . they are my inspiration.

Finally, for all those that have the courage to join me in the life of an entrepreneur, this book is dedicated to you.

SO YOU WANT TO BE AN ENTREPRENEUR?

Introduction

You've probably picked up, or been given this book, because you have an interest in becoming an entrepreneur, or maybe you just want to know more about these seemingly elusive individuals. Maybe someone has commented that you should be working for yourself or that you're the 'ideas man' or woman. Whatever your reason, you're in good company. Nowadays entrepreneurship is the new 'rock and roll'; everywhere you look there's a TV show or new book about it. Anyone would think it's a new idea or career, but in truth it's among the oldest. It's just going through a massive reinvention and now is a very good time to take a closer look.

For you and I, it's great news that this 'profession' is finally getting the break it deserves. We are now much more likely to get our ideas and plans heard, but in reality everyone benefits from a society that's rich in entrepreneurs. In my opinion, scarcely anything does as much for the progression of our society than entrepreneurship. Think about it; entrepreneurs are at the root of all of today's amazing technologies, economies and advances – right back as far as the invention of the wheel. Someone had to have the foresight to develop the idea to its practical application.

Whatever the reason for the 'new dawn' the profession is enjoying right now, it wasn't always this way. Not so long ago, people viewed entrepreneurs as slippery individuals who play fast and loose with other people's money. They were viewed with mistrust at best and certainly wouldn't have been given the kind of kudos that celebrated entrepreneurs in our society experience today.

'Entrepreneurs have arrived. Twenty years ago the word buccaneer would have come up, but now the definition of an entrepreneur is someone who is willing to take risks. We've improved our image quite a lot.'

Sir Stelios Haji-Ioannou
Founder and Chairman, easyGroup

With this new found respect, burgeoning entrepreneurs can take advantage of others' willingness to support and assist them in their endeavours. But let's not kid ourselves; it's as hard to be a success in this game today as it ever was, maybe even more so. With so many people increasingly attracted into the profession by its new glossy image, the unsuccessful amongst them (of which there are many) will frequently have one thing in common; they simply have no idea what they are getting into. The truth is being an entrepreneur is a very tough path. For those of you who remain unfazed by that; for those who even relish it, you are ready to delve a little deeper.

This book will guide you through a series of mentoring or coaching sessions, each designed to help you decide if this industry is suited to you. I don't intend to spend our time together just breaking down the skills and attributes of the most successful entrepreneurs. This has already been done ad nauseam. Whilst I will reference these things, this is really all about *you*. Together we will break down *your* lifestyle, traits and attributes and just as importantly; your potential to develop these things. Once we have done this, we will prepare you to take the next step, if indeed that's what you still want to do. I guarantee, you will be nothing if not prepared!

'Entrepreneurs are not born. Anyone can become one. It is a state of mind. And an approach to life. But if there is one core attribute that makes entrepreneurs different it is resilience. Great entrepreneurs do not panic, they survive. They view a great tactic as a strategy and opportunism as a positive.'

Doug Richard, *Dragons' Den*

Dreaming big dreams

'You look at things and ask – why?

but I dream of things that never were and ask – why not?'
George Bernard Shaw

Before we begin I would like you to think about your dream or vision in life. Do you have one yet? How can it motivate you? What does it say about you and what you should do with your life? Every successful entrepreneur I know is as curious as a cat and dreams big dreams – I don't mean vague daydreams but they have ideas and thoughts running through their heads all the time. Oftentimes, there is a single vision or dream sitting behind the continual stream of ideas.

So what's your big dream?

Dreamers are often dismissed as people with their head in the clouds. but dreams are an essential factor in the journey to becoming an entrepreneur, and beyond, so don't be put off. An entrepreneur creates the dream or vision and then rolls it over and over in his mind, shaping and cultivating it. This dream eventually becomes so clear and well defined that the entrepreneur will be willing to take risks, expend great quantities of energy, and work like heck to make it a reality.

Do you think your dreams are big enough and bold enough? Next time an idea or dream comes into your head, allow yourself to 'roll with it'. See where it begins to take you. Write it down and keep it close to you.

> *'The starting point of great success and achievement has always been the same. It is for you to dream big dreams. There is nothing more important, and nothing that works faster than for you to cast off your own limitations than for you to begin dreaming and fantasizing about the wonderful things that you can become, have, and do.'*
>
> **Brian Tracy,** *author of Eat That Frog series*

Following your dream

The only problem with dreaming big dreams is, you need to understand that this is just the beginning of the process. The difference between you and the daydreamer is that your dreams will progress and develop. They eventually grow wings and take flight, or at least they should if you are going to make a success of them – you must move to 'action' and not stop at the discussion stage. A great way to get the ball moving is to commit to an immediate action as soon as your dream looks feasible. Make a decision about progress (even if it's something simple like 'start researching the market') and then follow through with the first research-related call right away – don't wait. This will start the momentum.

INSIDER TIP

It's critical to get past talking and dreaming to some action, no matter how small, otherwise you can easily wind up with the other 99% who never achieve their dreams – always take immediate action at the point of a decision.

If I had to count the number of times people that I have met have told me their dreams about some next great blockbuster product or service, it would be in the hundreds. So, how many do I know that actually followed through – less than 1 in 20!

In fact, the following is a pretty typical example. I remember a dinner with a friend of my wife who worked for a very large business in a senior position. He was a little bored with life at work and had this 'fantastic' idea for a game he wanted to run past me. He explained in detail his idea for a board game. I think he had been tinkering with it for quite some time and even had a mock-up. He had obviously spent a lot of his spare time taking the basic idea to the first stage. He confirmed he had even done the 'due diligence' on the market and that it was all looking great. I wasn't sure how viable the idea was, but I admired the dream and was keen to follow his progress.

So, where is he now? Has his fantastic board game 'hit the shelves'? Has he waved goodbye to the corporate life in favour of the unpredictable yet rewarding life of an entrepreneur? Actually, when I checked back with him a year later I found out that he merely toyed around with the idea for months. It was a nice little hobby, but in reality he did little more than write up a short pitch for it.

What stopped this individual and the countless others like him from moving past the dreaming stage? It takes a leap of faith and lots of courage to go from a dream to action and then on to starting a business. He was in a nice, well-paid job with a pension, he had all the 'trappings' of the corporate world and he just couldn't take the essential jump from the comfortable office to the garage and a start-up.

Ironically, what holds some people back is exactly what motivates the next person. The pain of working for someone else can prove to be the greatest motivation of all, and is what finally persuades them to make the leap.

INSIDER TIP

You can harness any "pain or dissatisfaction" you are feeling to spur you to action. Don't avoid thinking about these emotions, use them to get leverage on yourself to get moving today.

It's a real inspiration when someone who dreams about working for themselves finally goes for it. *If they were to adopt a structured approach, making an inventory of all the personal and practical resources available to them, and they use this as basis for their business, they would be amazed at the results.*

A good example of this basic process in action is the story of Stuart Collingwood of Alba Fishing, a Scottish luxury fishing vacation business. Unlike you, he didn't have the advantage of a fully tried and tested approach to guide him through the early stages. He just followed his intuition.

Defining a dream

'Having become incredibly disillusioned with the software firm I was working for, I finally decided to make a clean break and follow a lifelong dream to set up my own business. This was not a calculated process, but actually came to me in a 'Eureka' moment whilst sitting on top of a mountain pondering my future. I simply wrote down all the components of what I enjoyed and had a talent for:

• dealing with people from all walks of life/cultures
• fishing
• knowledge and passion of the outdoors
• love of good food and cooking
• photography
• promoting the hidden secrets of Scotland
• talking business
• web marketing.

'Very quickly the idea presented itself to me. I literally ran down the hill and in less than a week had set up Alba Game Fishing Ltd. My main aim was to design and deliver a luxury fishing vacation experience, and include good food, photography on DVD and a 'can do' attitude to shaping trips for visitors.

'The early days of Alba were tough and it was hard to maintain a self-belief in selling a premium product when there are no orders in the book. My first few enquirers rejected the product as too highly priced and this made me wonder if I had made a great mistake. However, in the way that luck seems to favour the brave, an extensive article appeared in the *Daily Telegraph* the following week, entitled 'If you want to get ahead, get a rod'. It was all about how huge business deals were increasingly brokered on the river bank, not the golf course, and used William Daniel of *Famous Fishing* as the case study. Reading this gave me tremendous hope that I had to stay firm and hold out and that indeed it would all happen.

'The following week it did. I got my first booking – a retired lawyer from Kansas – and not long after that I was asked to look after the Poet Laureate Andrew Motion for two days. This proved to be key in pushing the business forward as Andrew wrote a very complimentary article in the *Daily Mail.* The article itself didn't produce any hard and fast bookings but I was able to close future business on this by sending the article as a PDF attachment along with the proposal.

'Three years on, the business has grown steadily and the new challenge is how to develop the next phase. We have launched a website in Russian and are launching online tackle sales in the winter. I also plan to introduce shooting to the business and have set up a new website offering similar packages to those of Alba Fishing.'

Stuart Collingwood, *Managing Director, Alba Fishing*

Stuart based his business on his dream, his passions and personal skill set. This gave him the drive to carry on when the road got tough. In much the same way, our sessions together will enable you to create a detailed inventory of your skills and passions. We will also get a better understanding of your lifestyle and personality to allow you to make the most informed decision.

Had he done this, our friend with the board game would have been better able to decide early on if he was suited to the life of an entrepreneur and if his idea filled him with enough passion and belief to see it through to its completion.

Your passion – what are you willing to do for the rest of your life?

'Live as if you were to die tomorrow. Learn as if you were to live forever.'

Mahatma Gandhi

One of the last things I am going to ask you to consider before we start our sessions together is your passion in life. What are you willing to do for the rest of your life? If you choose to be an entrepreneur, you must love what you do and have an intense passion for the dreams you are putting into play. If you haven't thought about it before, then now's the time to find your passion, find out what gets you leaping out of bed in the morning and focus on that as the start point for your decision about becoming an entrepreneur.

In my work with my mentees I actually start from this question, even before I hear about their idea or ambitions to be an entrepreneur – I always ask them to stop and tell me: 'What do you want from your life?' That question usually throws up a whole host of other questions; 'What sort of person are you? What would you love to do if you didn't have to earn a living or go to school? What do you want to be, feel or do?' 'What skills do you have?' 'Who do you know?' 'What resources do you have?'

INSIDER TIP

Stop thinking about the next super widget you want to launch to the unsuspecting public or whatever (if you already have a business idea). "Park" those ideas for now and start the process afresh with a search for your passion. Then compare one with the other to start on the right path to success.

What I am trying to find out is if they will be matched to their ambitions in the business they want to start. Later on, when we identify their business idea, I frequently find that it will <u>not</u> deliver what they actually need from it. It's so critical to 'do what you love' as far as you can in life – this is <u>doubly</u> true of starting or running your own enterprise, as it so much more challenging than working for someone else, and you will need every ounce of that passion and commitment when things get tough . . . and things will frequently get tough in the early days.

'If you choose a subject that you like and enjoy, the journey will be a much happier one and the chances of success much higher. Ask yourself if you would be happy working for your own company on Saturday at 1a.m. in the morning while all your friends are out partying. If the answer is "no" or even "oh well, yes if I had to", get yourself a nice, stable, salary-paying job.

'Working for yourself involves very long hours and you will be much happier if you enjoy what you are doing.'

Dr Jan Hruska
Co-Founder, Sophos

You are just about ready to join your first mentor session. Hopefully you will have begun to understand the value of letting yourself dream big dreams and appreciate that this is a powerful tool only when you follow it through, building and developing those dreams. Finally you will have begun to think about what it is that you could see yourself doing for the rest of your life, what passions you have in life.

Many people dream of starting a business but are hesitant to do so because they don't know if they're the right sort of person or are worried that they'll start a business and fail. I

INSIDER TIP

The *MONK and the RIDDLE (the Art of Creating a Life while Making a Living)* by Randy Komisar is a parable about having the 'juice' to make a success of your business, how to get a deep-down visceral drive for what you do.

It's one of my favourite books on the topic, and acts as a great inspiration to anyone thinking of embarking on a life of self-employment.

have devised a quick quiz to help you start to identify your entrepreneurial strengths and weaknesses.

Remember, life is a lot more complicated than just taking a test to predict the outcome of your success in business, and of course you shouldn't rely on the results in their entirety. The idea is to give you a 'pointer' as to you how you currently measure up to those traits already known to be consistent in successful entrepreneurs. Fill it out as honestly as possible and I'll see you in our first mentoring session for the beginning of a truly exciting and enlightening journey.

The entrepreneur test – is starting a business right for you?

(Take this quiz online for faster and more comprehensive results at: www.tobeanentrepreneur .com)

Please choose the two people in your life whose perception and judgment of you are most reliable. These are people who have known you for a long time, have your best interests at heart, but are not biased or afraid to tell you the truth as they see it. Decide now who these two people are and write them down in the box as A and B.

This quiz has been carefully designed by a psychotherapist, so it may seem a little 'different' – but follow the logic and you will get much more realistic results.

Person A (e.g. your partner)	Person B (e.g. your best friend)

Now in the following, *you* are person X – from now on, wherever it says X in the text, substitute your name.

Exercise 1:preparation
Take a moment and imagine you are person A. Imagine you enter their body and join into their experience: you look through their eyes, think through their brain, breathe through their lungs and feel through their feelings. For now, continue being person A.

As person A, you look at X. What immediately comes to your attention about X? What are the outstanding features you notice about X?

As person A, tell X your perceptions and impressions of X.

What is X's greatest strength? What is their greatest weakness?

As person A, tell X what you think is their greatest strength and their greatest weakness.

Example – X's greatest strengths are her enthusiasm and love of life. As for weaknesses; well, she can be stubborn.

If X were running a business, would you invest in it? Why would you? Any reasons why you wouldn't?

As person A, tell X why you would and why you would not invest in them.

Example – I would invest in X as I know she would be careful with my money and would never ask for any unless she was sure she could build a good business. My only concern is that she has not run her own business before and I am not sure how well she would do as an entrepreneur.

OK, that's the 'brain warm up' over; do you get the hang of the process now?

Now leave person A's body and return to yourself. How do you respond to what you have heard? Did you hear anything unexpected? This is where you think a bit about how you have responded and see how this works using someone else, not yourself, to answer honestly and frankly. The more you really entered person A's experience, the more this exercise feels like a real interaction, giving you real feedback from which you can learn.

Now you are ready to take the quiz, which will take about 10 minutes. Adding up the figures for the evaluation will take about 5 minutes. When you have made sure that you will have at least half an hour of uninterrupted time, you are ready to start.

Go through the questions swiftly and give a quick 'gut reaction' – is X most or least like the statement.

Exercise 2: take the entrepreneur personality quiz
To begin with, take a moment and imagine you are person B. Again, imagine you enter their body and join into their

experience: you look through their eyes, think through their brain, breathe through their lungs and feel through their feelings.

For now, continue being person B.

As person B, you will be asked a series of 50 questions about X (remember, X is you through the 'eyes' of B – you are acting as B for this exercise). Just put the letters M or L in the boxes to the right.

X is most or least like the statement below	Most/ Least
In most things X does, s/he will keep going until it is completed.	
When X has set his/her mind on something, s/he continues even when there are obstacles.	
Once X sets an objective, s/he works towards it until the end of the day and then leaves it for another time if not complete.	
X is always full of new ideas and dreams.	
X is rather afraid of standing out from the crowd or sticking her/his neck out.	
X is a creature of habit and likes to do things in the same way that s/he is used to.	
X can be very single-minded and will then shut out all other needs and influences.	
When X pursues a sport or hobby s/he gives up if s/he doesn't do well the first few times at it.	
People readily confide in X and seek him/her out for advice or a sympathetic ear.	
X is not very good at deceiving and cheating and it bothers her/him for a long time afterwards when s/he does.	
X is open and enthusiastic about her/his ideas and opinions and shares them readily with other people.	

If X believes in something, s/he is easily knocked off course by the opinions of others.	
X tends to do things right the first time, s/he doesn't change his/her approach.	
Although s/he can be a dreamer at times, most of every day X is active and on the go.	
X seems to operate on the assumption that it is better to have tried and failed than never to have tried at all.	
X will often attempt to solve problems or fix things even though s/he does not have the skills for it.	
X frequently has to be spurred on and encouraged by me and others.	
X is happy to live his/her life without uncertainty and doesn't like making leaps of faith.	
Before X makes an important decision, s/he usually asks for feedback from people s/he respects.	
If X had to choose between paying herself/himself and a staff member, s/he will pay herself/himself first.	
X is methodical and strategic and usually has a plan of action before starting a project.	
X is suspicious that others may steal or appropriate his/her ideas.	
X usually finds it hard to stand up and talk to an audience.	
X seems to feel that s/he deserves the good things in life.	
On the whole people seem to understand X clearly and easily.	
X learns more readily by doing rather than studying and reflecting.	
X acts based on clear evidence and doesn't like to make decisions otherwise even if s/he has no choice.	
Beyond having a vague image, X is able to visualize future scenarios in quite some detail.	
X tends to honour her/his commitments and promises, even if it puts her/him out.	

X resorts to white lies occasionally in order to beat the competition.	
After making a decision, X sometimes wonders whether s/he made the right one.	
In order to get a good deal, X is likely to be economical with the truth.	
X gets easily frustrated if s/he doesn't receive immediate rewards for her/his efforts.	
X can get easily rattled by others and feels undermined or insecure when others disagree.	
Faced with a sudden change in plans, X can usually come up with several alternatives quickly.	
X seems to have an innate faith in life, that s/he will always land on her/his feet.	
X can get drawn into the detail of problems, losing the bigger picture.	
X is willing to take risks and bear the consequences.	
X can't openly challenge people and speak her/his mind.	
X is known to have made intuitive decisions, without much rational evidence, and on the whole they have worked out.	
X always looks for new ways of doing things and is a keen learner.	
X may make mistakes, but s/he does not get into thinking of herself/himself as a bad, deficient, incapable person.	
X tends to be focused on today rather than a long-term dream.	
X will sometimes miss a meal in order to finish what s/he are doing.	
X frequently questions received wisdom and ignores advice from authorities, preferring to do her/his own thing or find out for herself/himself.	
X tends to put her/his hobbies first and does not allow work interfere with them.	
X easily gets worried about money and financial security.	

After X has an idea s/he likes to think long and hard about it before getting it started.	
When things go wrong for X, or s/he experiences setbacks, it tends to spur her/him on and make her/him more determined.	
X is not keen on surprises, and gets irritated when s/he has to change her/his plans.	

Remember this is just for fun! It gives you quick snapshot of how you feel now, but there's no right or wrong – and most exciting of all, you can learn a great deal of the traits and things you need to know – so the idea is to get a quick health check now and learn as you go along with some focus on areas for improvement.

Now go to the answers section at the back of this book to work out your Entrepreneurial Quotient.

Better still just use the online version!

[This quiz was co-authored with Michael Soth. Michael Soth is an integral-relational Body Psychotherapist, trainer and supervisor (UKCP), living in Oxford, UK. He has been working for many years to bring the outdated theories and techniques of psychology and psychotherapy into the 21st century, to support individuals, groups and organizations. Details about his published writing and articles are available at www.soth.co.uk]

Before we start the rest of the book with your new found insights from the quiz, I should explain that we will be using an approach I have used for over ten years as a mentor and a coach. We will progress as if we were having sessions together, and to make the process easier and faster we will also be using a fictional character called 'Jane' as an example of how to complete the exercises.

Most of my mentees benefit hugely from listening to each others' stories, and the questions and stumbling blocks that others are grappling with. Indeed, many ideas are often triggered from listening to the plans and dreams of others.

INSIDER TIP

If you haven't already sign up to the great blogs and forums relating to entrepreneurship. These are great places to chat to others like you and share stories, ideas and useful information. See the web site for links.

It is important to note that Jane's business ideas and chosen direction happen to represent a very scalable operation or 'lifestyle business' (more of this later). She is not designed to act as a benchmark to which you should aspire. Your own ideas may be much bigger or much smaller than hers. Where you will benefit most from Jane is by observing how she draws from her own experience of deciding in which direction she wants to go, and how her strengths and weaknesses support or impede her chosen course.

You can jot your answers directly into the book alongside Jane's, but better still, download the exercises and forms directly from the following website, where you will also find additional learning tools and more great insights from successful entrepreneurs.

www.tobeanentrepreneur.com

Mentor Session 1

Introduction to Entrepreneurship

- Introduction and overview
- What is an entrepreneur?
- Research into entrepreneurs
- Top ten traits of entrepreneurs
- Lesson–how do you measure up so far?

Introduction

Welcome to your first mentoring seminar.

Whether you are embarking on your first career, have come to a career crossroads much later down the line or whether you fall somewhere in between, you will benefit greatly from these sessions.

Firstly, let me congratulate you for coming this far. You obviously care deeply about who you are and what you are going to do with your life. You would be amazed how many people never even get to that point.

This is not an 'all or nothing' education, however. Whether we finish our journey together with you feeling confident to begin your new life as an entrepreneur, whether you decide to remain happily just as you are, or you decide to find some other great organization to work for, you are going to understand yourself and your motivations in life with a new and invaluable clarity.

Let me first tell you a little about myself and my experiences. I am a successful working entrepreneur, and contribute a large proportion of my time to mentoring others eager to succeed in the entrepreneurial world. My own entrepreneurial roots go back as far as I can remember. I was always a bit of a maverick, even at school. Growing up, I lived in many countries and was exposed to many cultures and languages – this helped me become a keen and curious observer of life. I was always one of those people who had a knack for listening, even as a child when kids would often confide in me. Conversely, I was also quite shy and something of a 'loner'.

I learned early on, however, that I could make friends and help other people not through my personality but by my *contribution.* At that age I didn't have a word for it, but today it's my watchword and what I base much of my life around.

Over the last 20 years I have started over half a dozen businesses; indeed, today I still run three so I am very much a working entrepreneur. However, I take the time to actively help others through giving my time, my resources and my money – my favourite phrase to sum up my philosophy is *you get what you give* – I find the more I give out to others, the more help I get back. Don't think that my giving is driven by a desire to get something in return, it is not. I am just reporting a healthy consequence of my actions. If you 'give to get' you will not have the same results, I assure you.

INSIDER TIP

I find the more people I help, the more seem to help me. I also find that the harder and smarter I work the luckier I get. Finally the more passionate and enthusiastic I am I find I get the same response from others.

Try it, you will find the same!

Over the years I have mentored hundreds of people from every race, class and culture. I have done this in the UK and the US, with everyone from business school students, to friends, to business colleagues. I have done this as part of 'Digital Ventures' (www.digital-ventures.com) and also as part of team at the London Business School and Stanford University. I have seen ideas from camera stores to dairy farms, from software to restaurants. In every case I have to say the same simple learning applies – those that were the most successful and happy were those that followed their passion and dreamed big dreams!

Over the next eight sessions I will take you on a journey to discover what an entrepreneur really is, what the research tells us and what the prevailing myths are. I will give you an insight into what life is like for a working entrepreneur, providing stories and examples from talented entrepreneurs I have being lucky to come into contact with. Then, together we will look at the different areas of your life and carry out a personal assessment of your potential to successfully become, and prosper as, a working entrepreneur.

I want you to think about yourself in a way that you have never done before. Don't immediately create excuses why it won't work for you. I want you to grab this opportunity with both hands and give it your best shot. Be painfully honest and as open-minded as you can; the benefits are going to be huge, no matter what outcome you choose. This is not a passive learning experience, I need you to get stuck in, and question and record your own thoughts as we go along.

Let's get started on our journey, joining us will be our fic tional friend Jane. Grab a pen now and take a look at the web site to download the forms we will start using below www.tobeanentrepreneur.com. If you don't have web access try and take a copy of the page as you will need more space than is provided in the book to work effectively.

Together with Jane, take a quick look at this list of ten questions that will help you answer the ultimate question: Do you want to become an entrepreneur?

There is no right or wrong answer at this time; just write whatever comes into your head. Keep your list to hand. We will then revisit it towards the end of our time together with what I promise to be surprising results!

So take your pen and the downloaded sheet of questions and complete it quickly and honestly. Below is how Jane did it to give you some ideas and how to go about it.

Top ten ways to answer the ultimate question – do I want to become an entrepreneur?

Name: *Jane Toomey*
EQ Score: *68%*

1 What characteristics do you share with successful entrepreneurs?

At this point I think, very little. I work as a logistics manager for a local catering firm and don't get much of a chance to put my own ideas into action. Although, I do have lots of dreams and ideas, I am not the most gregarious or 'risk hungry' person you will ever meet – I don't think that sounds like an entrepreneur.

2 What are your reasons for wanting to become an entrepreneur?

I'm not sure I really do want to be an entrepreneur, I mean I like the idea of working for myself and I know I have good ideas but I need to understand more about what the lifestyle would actually entail.

3 How would your family and friends react to you becoming an entrepreneur?

Would it impact them very much if I chose to become an entrepreneur? I'm not sure. They know even less than I do about real entrepreneurs. I suppose they would worry about the risks involved and my mum would say 'let someone else take the headache of running the businesses.' My friends wouldn't believe I could do it!

4 What do you think your life would be like on a day-to-day basis?

I suppose no one day would be the same and I would have to attend a lot of meetings about funding and revenue but I know there will be much more to it. I'm tempted to say 'sit and count all my money' 'because they seem to be focused on making as much money as possible but again I may be surprised with the reality.

5 What do you think the downsides are and how would you cope with them?

From what I understand about entrepreneurs I think they tend to make a lot of money then lose it all and then build it up again- Can I cope with the risk of losing it all? I'm renting an expensive flat and it's not just me. I have promised to put my brother through college next year and he would suffer if it all went wrong. Entrepreneurs also seem like big egos who like to do it all themselves — I think I would miss support of team members around me supporting me, celebrating and commiserating with me.

6 What is your ultimate vision or goal ?

I don't really know yet . . . I would like a family and a job related to my love of cooking, recipes and good healthy food that allowed me lots of time to spend with loved ones.

7 What are your core personality traits?

I am not sure. I am good with people I guess and I am a good organizer. I also come up with good ideas but beyond that I am not sure. I also don't know if those skills would stand up on their own without the support of a big company around me.

8 What life stage are you at and how do you think this will affect your chances?

I am four years out of school. I never went to college because I did a summer job in a catering firm and they agreed to take me on as an assistant straight out of school. I have a real passion for food and catering in general and I think they spotted that. I have only worked for this one company and haven't seen much of the world. I think it might work against me. I have moved out of home and I am renting a flat—so I don't really own anything.

9 What resources do you have available to you?

That would be a problem I think. I have a very small amount of savings which were meant to go towards buying a flat. They wouldn't really be enough to start a business with. I don't think a bank would give me any money and my friends are all paying off college debts.

10 What can you see yourself doing for the rest of your life?

That is an easier question. I can see myself being around food, cooking and catering of some kind for the rest of my life. I don't know if that is the right answer but right now, there is nothing else.

Jane notes:

I feel a bit vague in my answers but I don't really know what it means to be an entrepreneur and I don't really know what I want to do with my life. Hopefully by the time I look at these questions again I'll know exactly what I am going to do next, whatever path I choose.

You can see that Jane is totally new to the idea of being an entrepreneur, a situation which may not apply to you; you may have started your journey already. Don't avoid these questions, however, as they will be very useful for you as you go through the mentoring sessions. Take the time to write down the answers on a separate notebook which you can use for making all the notes as we go along.

Top ten ways to answer the ultimate question – Do I want to become an entrepreneur?

Your name: **EQ Score:**

1 What characteristics do you share with successful entrepreneurs?

2 What are your reasons for wanting to become an entrepreneur?

3 How would your family and friends react to you becoming an entrepreneur?

4 What do you think your life would be like on a day to day basis?

5 What do you think the downsides are and how would you cope with them?

6 **What is your ultimate vision or goal?**

7 **What are your core personality traits?**

8 **What life stage are you at and how do you think this will affect your chances?**

9 **What resources do you have available to you?**

10 **What can you see myself doing for the rest of your life?**

Your notes:

Have you answered the questions as best you can? OK, let's move on and learn more about entrepreneurship.

What is an entrepreneur?

The age of the entrepreneur has now well and truly arrived. Twenty years ago the word *buccaneer* would have been used in the same breath as entrepreneur, but now the definition of an entrepreneur is, someone who is willing to take risks to launch a product or service successfully.

A popular misconception is that inventors and entrepreneurs are one and the same. This is not the case. An inventor creates something new. An entrepreneur assembles and then integrates all the resources needed – the money, the people, the business model, the strategy, and the risk-bearing ability – to transform the invention into a viable business. He or she is a person who organizes, operates, and assumes the risk for a business venture. They have a talent for homing in on opportunities and have the abilities needed to develop those opportunities into profit-making businesses

'It is a contradiction in terms to call yourself an entrepreneur when you're actually betting other people's money. Let's define the entrepreneur as someone who is willing to take a risk with their own capital. In other words, they have upside but they also have considerable downside.

'The other thing that unites us as entrepreneurs is a burning desire to be our own bosses.'

Sir Stelios Haji-Ioannou
Founder and chairman, easyGroup

Research into entrepreneurs

The recent surge of interest in entrepreneurship has resulted in more focused research, which serves to benefit us all.

Across the globe, recognition is finally being given as to the importance of entrepreneurship to society.

'Entrepreneurship is America's most important competitive advantage. It's what America does much better than any other advanced industrial nation.'
William Bygrave, Babson College

Whilst traditional research rarely focused on entrepreneurs as a distinct group, this is now changing. Academic researchers have begun to look at the entrepreneurial process as something quite different from starting a small business or managing an established company. Research points to the entrepreneur's ability to take calculated risks and to have an achievement orientation, a sense of independence, an internal locus of control and a tolerance of ambiguity.

Contrary to popular belief, studies have shown that an entrepreneur does not need specific inherent traits, but rather a set of acquired skills.

'Successful entrepreneurs have a wide range of personality types. Most research about entrepreneurs has focused on the influences of genes, family, education, career experience, and so forth, but no psychological model has been supported.'

'There is no evidence of an ideal entrepreneurial personality. Great entrepreneurs can be either gregarious or low key, analytical or intuitive, charismatic or boring, good with details or terrible, delegators or control freaks. What you need is a capacity to execute in certain key ways.' [1]

---

[1] William Lee, What successful entrepreneurs really do (Lee Communications, 2201, Pleasanton, CA)

This is good news for those of us who don't fit the stereotype, and I include myself in that. You don't have to have an elusive set of special genetic traits to be a successful entrepreneur, and what you do need can be acquired from speaking to experienced entrepreneurs and reading as much as you can get your hands on.

What the evidence does tell us is that as a group, they demonstrate a unique response to the world around them.

'They work hard and are driven by an intense commitment and determined perseverance; they see the cup as half full, rather than half empty; they strive for integrity; they thrive on the competitive desire to excel and win; they are dissatisfied with the status quo and seek opportunities to improve almost any situation they encounter; they use failure as a tool for learning and eschew perfection in favour of effectiveness; and they believe they can personally make an enormous difference in the final outcome of their ventures and their lives.'[2]

So, everything you need can be learned. However, there is a core set of traits that is found among many successful entrepreneurs that they may have acquired through experience or been lucky enough to have been gifted as a child. It's a useful exercise to look at these traits in some detail. Indeed, even though you didn't know it at the time, you were being compared with these when you did the quiz. They were all questions based on the following characteristics.

These are a set of characteristics that are available to anyone. The following is not drawn from scientific

---

[2] New venture creation, Jeffry A Timmons and Stephen Sinelli

research, but from 20 years of personal experience and observation into the consistent characteristics of successful entrepreneurs.

The top ten traits of successful entrepreneurs

There are certain qualities common to many entrepreneurs. It's safe to say that most successful entrepreneurs possess at least some, and probably the majority, of these characteristics. This is not exclusive to entrepreneurship. If you want to be successful in anything you will need a combination of these attributes. You will have to focus on developing the traits that you currently don't possess if you want to make the grade.

The thing about being someone extraordinary like you, someone who is pushing boundaries, is that all the usual challenges to a successful outcome become more extreme. Being an entrepreneur is the severest test of anyone's 'character' and that's the point. It's not your skills or your charm or your age/race/color or creed it's about you and your *internal* resources.

'Anyone who can face up to decision making can learn to be an entrepreneur and behave entrepreneurially . . . Entrepreneurship is a behaviour rather than a personality trait. In 30 years I have seen people of most diverse personalities and temperaments perform well in entrepreneurial challenges. Some entrepreneurs are egocentric and others are painfully correct conformists. Some are fat and some are lean. Some entrepreneurs are worriers and some are relaxed . . . some have great charm and some have no more personality than a frozen mackerel!'

Peter Drucker

1 Persistence

'Nothing in the world can take the place of persistence. Talent will not; nothing is more common than unsuccessful men with talent. Genius will not; unrewarded genius is almost a proverb. Education will not; the world is full of educated derelicts. Persistence and determination are omnipotent.'

Calvin Coolidge

In my opinion, there's no single quality or trait that's more important to being a successful entrepreneur. Persistence is what keeps you motivated when things aren't going the way you thought they would – and they rarely do. The dictionary defines *persistence* as two words, *persistent determination*; but I shall increase the list to *persistent determination, motivation and belief.*

Determination: Winners implement their ventures with total commitment. They seldom give up, even when confronted by obstacles that seem insurmountable.

Motivation: You must be willing to keep trying when things go wrong, and accept that, ultimately, it's up to you to make your dream come true. Motivation enables you to stick with your dream when the going gets rough; it has to come from within you.

Belief: You control your success or failure, and that it is not decided by luck, circumstance, or external events. Successful entrepreneurs have an enduring belief in themselves that gives them the capacity to recover from serious defeat or disappointment.

'If you want to be successful in a particular field or endeavour, I think perseverance is one of the key qualities.

It's very important that you find something that you care about, that you have a deep passion for, because you're going to have to devote a lot of your life to it.'

George Lucas

2 Confidence

'All you need is ignorance and confidence and the success is sure.'

Mark Twain

Together with persistence, you will need to start thinking about your confidence level. You've got to have a good measure of confidence in yourself, but also in other people and in your surroundings. Self-confidence is an essential trait in an entrepreneur, because you're regularly called upon to perform tasks and make decisions that require great amounts of faith in yourself. You need to have a strong but realistic belief in yourself and your ability to achieve your goals.

Mark Twain's seemingly contradictory quote highlights the fact that 'ignorance' actually goes hand-in-hand with confidence for many new entrepreneurs. They have no fear of the unknown, they just do it. In fact, if they knew what many people did they probably wouldn't attempt the fantastic feats they do, as so many successful entrepreneurs have done before them.

Without confidence it would be very hard to get that first investor to give you a start, or to encourage your first staff member to come on board, or to sell to the first customer. You will discover that confidence has a bearing on almost all the critical milestones in any venture's success.

3 Vision

'Vision is the art of seeing the invisible.'

Jonathan Swift

Entrepreneurs have a vision of what the future could be like for them and their businesses. And, more importantly, they have the ability to implement this vision or dream. Most great entrepreneurs have a strong desire to originate an idea or product, to develop something new, to be innovative and to make something happen. They want to imprint their dreams and ideas on a concept in a unique and different way. Often the idea can be pushing a boundary that society or industry has set, and it can't re-invent itself due its long history of operating in a particular way – that's where a paradigm shift can make you very successful. Richard Branson is a perfect example of someone who is constantly trying to change businesses from music, to airlines to mobile phones and now banking. In each case there was an opportunity to re-invent the business for the benefit of the consumer and as a result he could build a new and flourishing company in an old stagnant market!

4 Action

'Hatching an idea is only the beginning of the battle. The foundation for nearly every conspicuous American achievement, organization or institution was laid by the sweat and sacrifice and unconquerable perseverance of some man possessed by an idea he was willing to give his life for, if necessary. Don't make the mistake of imagining that an idea, no matter how good, can win its way in the world unless you have grit enough, backbone enough, enthusiasm enough to get behind it and push with all your might.'

Forbes, 1921

This is the trait that sets apart those with the dream from those that succeed. It's great to dream but you then need the ability to execute and turn the idea into reality and on to commercial viability. It's critical once you believe in an idea that you make the step to some form of action right away in order to start building momentum towards your goals. 99% of budding entrepreneurs fail at this; they talk a good game but do not follow through. Winners decide on a course of action and they implement it as quickly as possible.

Once you do get started, being an entrepreneur is all about getting things done, usually against the odds. It is about setting goals and exceeding them. Rather than being content with reaching goals, successful entrepreneurs continue setting new goals to challenge themselves. They don't procrastinate. They make decisions swiftly and this swiftness is a key factor in their success.

5 Dedication

'The price of success is hard work, dedication to the job at hand, and the determination that whether we win or lose, we have applied the best of ourselves to the task at hand.'
Vince Lombardi

No 'ordinary' amount of action is required to succeed; it requires your total dedication.

This dedication will be a combination of stamina, passion and commitment. A high level of stamina is essential in allowing you to meet the intense demands of running a business along with single-mindedness that will drive you until you reach your goal.

Winners give everything to their business right from its conception, sometimes at considerable cost to their relationships with their friends and families. They work tirelessly and with a tremendous amount of passion. Passion is particularly important for entrepreneurs because, although rewarding, the process of starting and building a new firm is demanding. Twelve-hour days and seven-day weeks are not uncommon when an entrepreneur is striving to get a business off the ground.

Of course, this dedication must stem from a place of love or it is simply unsustainable. Entrepreneurs must love what they do. It is that love that drives them and gives them the energy to be totally dedicated when the going gets tough.

6 Faith

> *'All the strength and force of man comes from his faith in things unseen. He who believes is strong; he who doubts is weak. Strong convictions precede great actions.'*
> **James Freeman Clarke**

Most successful people in general, as well as entrepreneurs, have had to take a leap of faith in their venture at some point to avoid defeat. They have to go the extra mile when all else seems lost. A well-known and powerful little poem best illustrates this point:

> *If you think you are beaten, you are;*
>
> *If you think you dare not, you don't;*
>
> *If you'd like to win, but think you can't it's almost a cinch you won't;*
>
> *Life's battles don't always go to the stronger or faster man;*
>
> *But soon or late the man who wins is the one who thinks he can.*
> **Walter D. Wintle**

As an entrepreneur, there will be many times when you will have to have to demonstrate faith in your idea, your colleagues, your family and yourself. But you will need to go beyond the logical acceptance of the need for faith to actually finding it – it is not a tangible thing. Faith requires that you reflect and consider your position and then continue against all the logical evidence because you believe in your dream.

Do not confuse belief with faith.

> *'Faith is not belief. Belief is passive. Faith is active.'*
> **Edith Hamilton**

7 Integrity

> *'The supreme quality for leadership is unquestionably integrity. Without it, no real success is possible, no matter whether it is on a section gang, a football field, in an army, or in an office.'*
> **Dwight David Eisenhower**

This may seem a less obvious trait in the list but I believe it's one of the most powerful ways to succeed in the long term.

As the life of an entrepreneur is a long term game, it pays to live your life by strong principles and not to compromise these in order to achieve your goals. 'You get what you give' is one of my touchstone phrases and a great mantra to live your life by.

You will have many opportunities take shortcuts along the road to entrepreneurial success but it rarely pays to do so. Those that are honest and treat others with respect and fairness will be the ultimate winners. Experience has taught me that people will follow a person with true integrity into the wilderness and beyond, whereas a leader without morals will soon be alone when the money runs out.

8 Adaptability

'All fixed set patterns are incapable of adaptability or pliability. The truth is outside of all fixed patterns.'

Bruce Lee

A truly successful entrepreneur is totally flexible in the achievement of their outcome. They are receptive to change, can adjust perceptions, goals or action based on an assessment of new information.

One of the great benefits of a small or early stage business is the ability to change rapidly, often much faster than the competition. You may have to change your basic idea based on customer feedback. You may have to rethink the way you deliver a product; your go-to-market strategy; your sales method or one of the many of the other factors that affect success. The people involved in the journey with you will also need to change and adapt with you, the entrepreneur.

Coupled with adaptability is versatility. You will need to be capable of dealing effectively with many subjects or tasks at the same time, along with being able to assume different roles, and to switch back and forth as required.

9 Courage

'Success is not measured by what you accomplish, but by the opposition you have encountered, and the courage with which you have maintained the struggle against overwhelming odds.'

Orison Swett Marden

As an entrepreneur, you will need to be able to face your fears and take action. You will have to overcome countless odds and believe me; it will pay to have nerves of steel. So many people fail when they are required to show their mettle. In order to succeed you need to be able to find the internal resources to make the tough decisions along the road.

Successful entrepreneurs will often have had to give up their jobs to embark on a new venture. Deciding to risk the unknown, at the expense of a regular salary and benefits such as health insurance, pension plans and paid vacations takes immense courage.

In addition, the prospective entrepreneur frequently has to face friends, family, and maybe a spouse who do not always understand or support his or her desire for self-employment, with all its risk and uncertainty, and its drain on their time, energy, and resources. With sustained courage and conviction, you'll be surprised at how often things work out even better than you had ever expected them to.

10 Communication

'*Certainly a leader needs a clear vision of the organization and where it is going, but a vision is of little value unless it is shared in a way so as to generate enthusiasm and commitment. Leadership and communication are inseparable.*'

Claude Taylor

All of the traits we have discussed in this session would be pretty redundant without the ability to get your message across to all the relevant parties. If you cannot inspire, enthuse, motivate and excite people about your dreams then they will be much harder to achieve.

Excellent communication skills are critical in enabling you to interact well with people of varying personalities and values, many of whom will not necessarily share your passion or motivation. You will need to communicate yourself out of the many roadblocks you will meet along the way, from financing and legal issues, to recruitment, and to simply helping people 'get' your idea. It all requires your ability to communicate effectively.

INSIDER TIP

Selling and great communication abilities are not a "dark art" for people who love to talk. I am an introvert who had to teach himself to sell and to talk to people persuasively and you can too, there are lots of great books, DVDs and inexpensive courses on the these topics.

Don't worry if you don't feel like you have these skills, you can easily learn them!

As such you must also be a consummate sales person. You must be able to use words and explain concepts effectively and persuasively, both verbally and in writing. You also need the ability to present proposals clearly to influence bankers or investors to supply money. Your communication skills will also be called upon in your dealings with employees, to help them understand the exact nature of their job and the results you expect, and also to encourage customers to buy from you.

The candidates most likely to be successful entrepreneurs will have some or all ten of the traits discussed–how do you measure up? You are not expected to possess a complete and polished set from the outset but, can you see yourself with these characteristics or do you think you could learn them?

I suggest you now think about your quiz results again now that you know the different areas the questions relate to. Thinking about these traits; now do you feel you can integrate them into your life? Whether you ultimately see yourself as an entrepreneur or not, you will undoubtedly find they boost your personal and professional success.

> Find a copy of all the lessons and forms for you to use on our website www.tobeanentrepreneur.com

Lessons

Based on your learning of these entrepreneurial traits, complete this checklist:

How you measure up (rank from 1–5, with 1 being least like you and 5 being a strong match to you)

	Personality trait	Your answers	Jane's answers
1	Persistence		3
2	Confidence		4
3	Vision		2
4	Action		4
5	Dedication		3
6	Faith		3
7	Integrity		4
8	Adaptability		2
9	Courage		2
10	Communication		4

Now choose out of the ten traits which are the following:

Your answers:		
Least like you	**More like you**	**Strong match to you**

Jane's answers:		
Adaptability	Persistence	Confidence
Courage	Dedication	Action
	Faith	Communication
	Vision	Integrity

Notes

Refer back to the quiz at the beginning and now think about the ten traits and your ability to develop or work on areas you are less strong in.

In the box below make any notes that are relevant to you and what you have learned so far.

My notes on what I have learned:

Jane's:

Poor on adaptability and courage. Not sure how that will impact me. We'll have to wait and see!

Once again don't give up if these things look difficult for you – add them to your formula for success. Be positive. If you are not happy with some of these things, note them down – then do what I do; find the additional resources to complement your skill set when the time comes.

Now let's consider some other entrepreneurial qualities.

Of course, it's not as simple as ticking the box in a list of entrepreneurial characteristics in order to understand if you are ideal material!

Life is way to complex for that and so are entrepreneurs.

So to explore in more detail ask yourself the following:

Are you the type of person that likes to bend the rules?

I often find (as has research) that entrepreneurs like to' change the game'. They like to re-make the rules to give them an advantage. I find myself doing this all the time. For example, if a big company gives me an order and insists on their terms of business I will always try and make them compromise in a way that suits me, like faster payment terms. Most corporate-minded people wouldn't think it possible with a big company, or just wouldn't bother asking.

You will find again and again that you will need to be looking for ways to buy at a better price, to agree better terms or win an order against the odds. Another good example is when I secured an order with a big corporate and I didn't even have an office! I made a great website, talked the talk, looked good and gave a strong presentation as to our company's skills (which I truly believed in, by the way) – and all while we were a start-up with nothing behind us. That's 'chutzpah', or bottle, and you will need it to win if you plan to build a business against the odds.

INSIDER TIP

Don't be afraid to re-shape the world as you see it to suit you. Many people feel like they have to do things like they used to when they worked for another company or they are shy about getting better terms when working with bigger companies.

Don't be – they are not better than you, you make the rules now, do business in the most advantageous way you can.

Don't forget this may not be you; you may have a team member who can do this for you.

Are you prepared to bootstrap your business and grow patiently?

Time and again I have started a business with little or no money. Even now that I do have money I still don't waste any of it; I always bootstrap and start slowly. This can be very frustrating, but a lean approach will always pay off because it breeds prudence and patience, helping you build a truly sustainable business and outlast the competition.

This becomes even more relevant when you think about how many people have to borrow or sell part of their company to grow – the less you borrow or sell the faster you will make a profit and the more you will own of the business when it's a success.

Do you have the guts to find the funds when you are up against it? Many times I have had to get a bank loan, borrow up to my limit on credit cards or sell a favourite item to keep the cash flowing–will you do that when your back's against the wall?

INSIDER TIP

Many people forget that not only do you need to be good at selling, you also need to be great at buying and negotiating with suppliers. Great entrepreneurs are often as good at this (i.e. saving money) as they are at promoting their businesses.

"Every penny saved is a penny earned".

Are you prepared to take on the 'big boys' to win?

Once again you will need courage and maybe even a little bravado. I often find myself playing David in a market full of Goliaths. I personally love this as it gives me an 'angle' when approaching new clients, i.e. as a smaller player I'm ready to serve and assist my new customers more effectively than the slow and inefficient competition.

Now don't get me wrong, I rarely try and provoke the bigger and meaner competition. Usually I look for a chink in their armour – maybe a niche market they have under-served or overlooked. All the while I exploit my position to get customers to choose me over a bigger rival, using a range of tactics from clever public relations to being able to undercut on price. I'm never afraid of taking on bigger competitors. In fact, it's often part of a strategy to make them buy me out of a market as I have become a thorn in their side!

INSIDER TIP

Make sure you do detailed 'homework' on your competitors. Many people are lazy and don't take the time to fully understand the competition and therefore often miss great opportunities or get easily crushed.

Are you prepared to be flexible and reshape your dream based on customer reality?

Many people work so hard on a particular dream business idea, they become wedded to it. I have found this to be a big mistake. Almost all of my business ideas have had to change at least once after I have gone out and spoken to real customers. In one example, I started a business based on an idea I had gleaned from a business trip in the US in the pre-internet days, called 'fax on demand'. It was very popular in the US and I thought I could do the same in the UK, so I launched a business and bought all the expensive gear. After a year of only having sold a few systems, all I got from customers was, 'that's nice, but what about this new internet-stuff?' So one painful day I disposed of all the expensive gear, changed the name of the business and started out down the path of a web design . . . and a pretty successful business it was too.

Now if I hadn't made the expensive decision to give up on my first idea and respond to customer demand, I would have gone out of business rather than building a successful one. You must be prepared to try an idea in the real world and keep tailoring it until you find the right formula for your customers. Become totally focused on satisfying their needs and not your own ego and you will have a much better chance of success.

One of the great keys to business success is to constantly read the market and make sure you steer your 'ship' along with the greatest flow of opportunity.

Don't be afraid to give up older ideas and markets to pursue new ones, otherwise you massively increase the risk of failure.

Can you get knocked down and keep getting up?

One of the hardest things for new entrepreneurs is the constant 'no, no, no . . .' you will hear from everyone about everything! People will reject your idea, your plan, your phone calls, your pleas for money or help. You will get knocked back more times than you will be able to remember. You will need to endure this, day in day out, and still be able to get back up and try again the next day. The chances are, one day you will fail all together and your business will no longer exist. Will you be able to get started again – get back on the horse?

Remember, it's not all bad, If you are persistent enough you will find lots of people willing to listen, help you and push you towards your dreams – but you will have to fight to convince those people.

Will you be a fighter and roll with the punches?

Being persistent is critical to any form of success but if you are in a startup it's more important than anything else in my view.

What's great about it is that you don't need to learn it, you simply must 'decide' that you will make your dream work no matter the odds.

After that it's quite easy – don't give up and you will come out the winner!

Entrepreneurs Uncovered

- Top ten myths about entrepreneurs
- What makes people become an entrepreneur?
- Are you feeling like an entrepreneur yet?
- Lessons

In our last session we got to grips with what the research says about entrepreneurs and what behaviours and traits are consistent in the most successful entrepreneurs. You will have started to measure yourself against these things and have some idea of the areas you need to work on and develop. Are you feeling more or less motivated by what you learning about yourself? Don't judge your reactions, just be aware of them.

In this session we're going to discuss the prevailing myths about entrepreneurs, and there are many – believe me. I'll also give you an insight into the reasons people choose this road and what real life is like for an entrepreneur.

Let me start by saying that many of the myths are just plain wrong and appear to be invented by those unprepared to take the risks themselves, or who are envious of the rewards a lucky few get after years of hard labour. The media don't help by showing kids getting venture capital funding during the dot-com boom and quickly striking it rich; as this is not the reality most entrepreneurs live by and such events are the exception rather than the rule.

Top ten myths about entrepreneurs

1 Entrepreneurs are born, not made

This is the biggest myth, so let's dispel it right away! Sure, some people are more likely to become entrepreneurs if their parents have made a success of it, or if they have witnessed another family member working for themselves – but it's not down to genes. In fact, many who see what a tough life it can be go in the other direction and take steady jobs.

It should be clear to you now that you can acquire the right technical skills and mindset to become an entrepreneur through education and experience. One key thing you must develop from the outset is the drive, ambition and courage to see your venture through – but don't worry, if you are following your dream and basing your business on what you love, you will find these things come naturally!

2 Entrepreneurs are well educated, rich and young

This is the media at work again. Let's look at the facts. Who do you know who is starting a business? They're probably in their forties or older (many surveys have proved this to be the average age). They don't tend to be MBA graduates, either. In fact, so many successful entrepreneurs have little formal education that it's now become something of a slogan for entrepreneurs.

And rich . . . well, having money may make life a little easier for getting capital, but it can often lead to lack of 'fire in the belly' needed to take the risks required to succeed. In today's world you can succeed with a healthy amount of common sense, very little money and start at any age you like as long as you have the energy to push your idea into the world.

3 Entrepreneurs are big gamblers

Experienced entrepreneurs are <u>not</u> generally big gamblers. Of course, there are times when you have to take a significant risk, but that's rare. Most entrepreneurs attempt to minimize the risk of a new opportunity by calculating the consequences of their decisions before they implement them.

The idea that entrepreneurs are inherently risk-takers is down to a number of things. The fact that their lives appear to be more carefree and unstructured gives the impression of a life of constant risk, as does striking out into the unknown without the safety net of an employer. This impression is reinforced by high profile, failed entrepreneurs featured in the media.

It's a fact of course that going it alone is more likely to end in failure, but frankly, with adequate preparation it's not that much more risky than getting fired from your job. Entrepreneurs do not deliberately seek to take unnecessary risk, but nor do they shy away from unavoidable risk.

4 Entrepreneurs are loners and cannot work with others

Donald Trump and Richard Branson may appear to be loners and autocrats, but the reality is that their success is down to a core team of managers working for them and executing their ideas. It's true that many of us will start out alone with our idea but again, if we are experienced, we soon look to create a strong team around us to help get the idea off the ground. "Two heads are better than one", and while strength of character and courage are often needed from the entrepreneur to get things started, things won't get that far without a high quality management team.

Most entrepreneurs will actively seek the advice of others and will make many business contacts to validate their business ideas. The most successful entrepreneurs are leaders who build great teams and effective relationships working with peers, directors, investors, key customers and important suppliers.

The entrepreneur who is a 'loner' and will not talk to anybody will never start a successful business. One of the key reasons is that most businesses need funding. The number 1 reason why businesses get funded is the quality of the team behind the business – one man is not generally enough.

5 Entrepreneurs only care about money

It would be wrong to say that most entrepreneurs are in it for the money, because so many could make more if they went back to work in their former jobs. Almost all are driven by other reasons. Of course, everyone would like to be wealthy and live a good life. Indeed, it would be fair to say that many entrepreneurs are competitive and use their ability to generate wealth as a way to keep score, but anyone who just does a job for the money won't stick at it for long or will end up poor.

Much more motivating for the entrepreneur is the sense of personal achievement and pride, along with feeling in control of their own destinies, and the reward of realizing their vision and dreams. Money is viewed as a tool and a way of keeping score, rather than an end in itself. Entrepreneurs thrive on the thrill of the chase. Often, even after an entrepreneur has made a few million pounds/ dollars or more, he or she will get right down to work on the next new vision.

> 'Ridiculous yachts and private planes and big limousines won't make people enjoy life more, and it sends out terrible messages to the people who work for them. It would be so much better if that money was spent in Africa – and it's about getting a balance.'
>
> **Richard Branson**

6 Most successful entrepreneurs start their companies with a break-through invention or technology

It's true that these types of entrepreneurs get the most 'air-time', but if you look at the facts, the glamorous and inventive ideas are great but not the cornerstone of the world economy. Usually it is the simple things in our daily lives that get reinvented or improved. This reinvention is the core of most entrepreneurial activities. Indeed, even the blockbuster products like the iPod were actually improvements on someone else's original idea and design.

The trick is spotting an opportunity to improve something, offer it at a better price or delivery mechanism or fill a gap in the market. There are opportunities a plenty in so many parts of our lives, so there's no need to emulate Bill Gates to get ahead as an entrepreneur. In fact, research shows that most entrepreneurs are not basing their business on technology-based services or products – so you don't need to either, unless that's your thing.

7 Fail at your first business and you will never get a second chance

Firstly, you will soon learn that it may well take a few tries at life as an entrepreneur before you have your first real success. Almost all entrepreneurs have to learn on the job, because even the best business schools can only ever teach you the theory. The chances of success are always slim, and experienced investors and entrepreneurs know this.

They key thing is to "fail well" – that is to learn from the experience and to act with integrity. Try not to let staff and suppliers down. Be honest and open. If you do fail, the people that matter will respect you for trying your best. What's more, if you are not playing fast and loose with their funds, they are likely to come back to you, as you are much more likely to succeed after having tasted failure.

'It doesn't matter how many times you fail. It doesn't matter how many times you almost get it right. No one is going to know or care about your failures, and neither should you. All you have to do is learn from them and those around you because . . . all that matters in business is that you get it right once. Then everyone can tell you how lucky you are.'

Mark Cuban Billionaire internet entrepreneur and professional basketball team owner

8 They couldn't get a good job so they work for themselves

This may appear true, as many entrepreneurs are not ideal employees for the very reasons that they are good entrepreneurs; but in reality, the majority of new entrepreneurs have worked for a company for many years before they took the plunge. The experiences they gained from their jobs gave them both the skills as well as the ability to spot opportunities. When they don't have the direct experiences, clever entrepreneurs will often get a job in a type of business they intend to launch to find out all about the operational, financial and other issues behind the business.

Then, once you do start a venture you will need to stick at it for 5–7 years for an average business, to get a decent return on your investment of time, money and sweat. So, in reality most entrepreneurs will be in this game out of choice or opportunity. That said, in today's unstable world, many of us will be forced into working for ourselves if the corporate machine fails, leaving us with a family to feed – and that's good enough motivation for starting your own business in my book!

9 Entrepreneurs have to sail very close to the wind to succeed

Once again the media hasn't done the world of entrepreneurship many favours. In the past, entrepreneurs were represented in sitcoms and film as the rogue trader/artful dodger type. Now we have reality TV showing people stepping all over each other to become apprentice entrepreneurs. Once again, both representations are misleading. Sometimes as an entrepreneur you may be tempted to compromise the letter of the law or your personal integrity, but every time it will be a mistake. Much like the person that becomes an entrepreneur for the money, you will fail.

Of course, you may have to be a little 'innovative' at times and pretend to be a little bigger and better than you are to impress the first client, but you should never willingly mislead, as it will always end in tears. Your reputation will be the most valuable thing over the years, and you need to protect it.

10 You will have no life as an entrepreneur

All successful entrepreneurs work long hours, at least in the early years. But that's no different to any corporate manager in today's world. The great benefit of being an entrepreneur is that, in time, you can pick and choose how you structure your life around yourself and not your boss. After you have created a stable business you can actually decide how and where you spend your time, and many entrepreneurs have incredibly flexible lives that work around their family needs and schedules.

In my experience my time is my own and I work and live my life according to whatever schedule suits me that day. This means that if I want to go to my son's soccer match during the day, that's what I will do and then work into the evening. It's that flexibility that is one of the perks of the job, but you will have to work long hours to pay for that luxury.

What makes people become an entrepreneur?

A Global study[3] into entrepreneurial activity showed that individuals start a business for two main reasons:

1. They want to exploit a perceived business opportunity (opportunity entrepreneurs).
2. They are pushed into entrepreneurship because all other options for work are either absent or unsatisfactory (necessity entrepreneurs).

The vast majority of early-stage entrepreneurs across the world claim that they are attempting to take advantage of a business opportunity.

Most entrepreneurs that I know became so because they were fed up with being 'told what to do', and wanted to strike out on their own with all the freedom that goes with being your own 'boss'.

Not that many start out just for the money (and that's lucky as there is not usually much going around); but for the ability to make a difference in their own and other's lives.

Most think they have spotted a gap in the market, think they can do it better than their former employer or have come up with a new product or service they believe will be a winner. These people are often naturally aware of opportunities, and when they recognize ideas for new products or services, they have a desire to turn those ideas into reality.

Of course, a huge number will have an idea or see a problem that needs to be addressed when working for their employer,

[3] Global Entrepreneurship Monitor, 2006 results, Niels Bosma and Rebecca Harding, http://www.gemconsortium.org

but cannot get any traction where they are; and because of their passion and commitment, some employees choose to leave the firm employing them in order to start their own business as the means to develop their own ideas.

It will be obvious that the reasons why people start a business, or become an entrepreneur, are as wide as there are types of people and opportunities.

From research, the most often cited reason for doing so is to 'be their own boss' – or in other words, they wanted independence and freedom. Of course, you can expand that concept to include many things like pursuing their own ideas or projects, looking for a better life and hopefully more financial rewards for their efforts.

Many will leave just because they are unhappy with their job, or the employment options available at the time, or they have harboured a need to start their 'own thing' and have been waiting for the right project. (Be careful not to interpret being bored or disillusioned with your job as an automatic trigger to becoming an entrepreneur; you may just need a new challenge in another corporate environment.)

Beyond this, some people, through a hobby, leisure activity, or just everyday life, recognize the need for a product or service that is not available in the marketplace.

Unfortunately you may be made redundant, or otherwise find yourself forced out into the job market. These are appropriate times to reflect and consider being an entrepreneur too (although you should think carefully about making any snap decisions because your ego has been dented).

Finally, people may start their own firms to build a better life with better potential rewards. As I have said before, this tends to be a secondary issue in reality, because such people usually have a burning desire to get started that comes well above actually chasing money. We all hope that our ideas will be popular and allow us to improve our lifestyles, but this is simply a by-product of success and not the prime motivation.

In my case I started up my first business right out of college because I thought it would be fun with a friend. I was only eighteen and we had a great time. Worked hard, made some money and had fun until we fell out! Then I went to work in a 'proper job' until I was 26 when I started out again after being made redundant from a high-powered job. So I have jumped off and on the job ladder. I did it at first as it felt right and the second time because it looked more interesting than getting another corporate position. I wanted the freedom and I wanted to be rewarded directly for my own efforts. I have never looked back!

I do have to admit that during my time in gainful employment I really didn't fit in that well. I didn't enjoy working for other people, especially those I didn't respect. I found that those for whom I did have respect kept getting moved or fired, leaving me with my next egotistical and uninspiring boss! As you can tell I was not ideal corporate material and so I always had jumping off the ladder in the back of my mind.

So there is no set pattern in peoples' motivations. Just look at what you need from your life and see if entrepreneurship is right for you and right for you now. Do you have a strong enough motivation to change your life?

Are you feeling like an entrepreneur yet?

We have looked at some of the qualities and myths and lifestyle of an entrepreneur in a very general way. There are countless traits and foibles of entrepreneurs that we haven't yet looked at, but that's OK, because what I'm simply trying to do is to give an indication – is this for you? Having read about their attributes, you shouldn't try and force yourself into a character that you visualize, but simply say on balance – are these qualities that I have, or could develop or feel comfortable with? Or not, as the case may be.

Your energy, passion, commitment and drive will be what make you a successful entrepreneur or not, much more than any skills, resources or formal education. You must judge your personality carefully before choosing either an entrepreneurial or executive career. The insights of family, friends and associates can also be really helpful in this process.

INSIDER TIP

When you get feedback from people about you they will not want to say anything "bad" so you need to very clear that you need them to be totally honest.

For the same reason it can be useful to ask people you know less well or those you can trust to be blunt or the process will be a waste of time.

Your learning so far should have highlighted some of your areas of personal development and the degree to which you will need to make changes if you want to pursue an entrepreneurial career. Be careful, though, to assess whether the change is worth the personal cost. It is far better to make an honest judgment from the outset, decline the opportunity, and avoid the potential personal, financial, and career risks.

Remember that practically anyone can become an entrepreneur with the right drive and passion. If you are unsure if you possess the traits and behaviour discussed so far, don't give up; you probably need a reality check from someone who knows you, a trusted friend or family member. Go ahead and ask them – I bet they will say you either have the traits to some degree or you could develop them!

If you want to start a business or become an entrepreneur you should. Don't let anyone put you off or discourage you, it's not the reserve of the 'chosen ones'. **Anyone can do it.**

Have you downloaded the forms yet? Go here now: www.tobeanentrepreneur.com

Lessons

Myths about entrepreneurs – personal learning

Yours:

Jane's:

Wow! It's amazing how inaccurate the general perception about entrepreneurs is. Most of the reasons why I personally thought the entrepreneur life wouldn't suit me, turned out to be false. Firstly I don't have to be well-educated and rich, in fact many of the top entrepreneurs dropped out of school. Secondly, they don't do it by themselves as I had assumed. They have teams around them to complement their skills. I can find the people with the skills I'm not so big on! They don't set out to find risky situations to gamble *their life away on, they take calculated risks. Neither is it the end of the world if I was to fail first time, this can actually work to my favour. Finally they are not, as I thought, in pursuit of the mighty dollar. They see this as a by-product but not the end game. Hmm — I'm quickly running out of excuses. However, I need to start looking about closer at my lifestyle, experience and resources.*

Just for fun – try asking your friends and family what they think about when they think of entrepreneurs. Try and dispel some of those myths.

Why not ask them how they think you measure up to some of the top ten traits of successful entrepreneurs? Record your findings here:

Family	Friends	Colleagues
Your friends/family views:		

Family	Friends	Colleagues
Jane's:		
Talked to dad about the important traits for entrepreneurs. He did say that I am one of the most persistent people he knows — I was really surprised.	Mark thinks I have great vision when I can bounce ideas off someone, we decided with a little help from a team I can be quite the visionary!	I didn't want to tell them what I was doing, so I went back through all my old appraisals and discovered communication really is a strong point of mine — great!

Mom says I am often a bit scared to try new things. I don't think I have had a chance to prove I have courage but I had rated it least like me when I did the exercise anyway.	Carol, a family friend who knows me since I was little, says I don't adapt to change very well. She did say that I am a real 'do-er' and am confident in my decisions.	
Dad says I am really persistent. I was surprised as I didn't think it was one of my strong points.		
As an aside Dad said he thought I'd struggle with the 'bootstrapping' bit — I think he underestimates my ability to not buy shoes.		
"Make a few notes about what you have now learned from the feedback above. See Jane's notes to help below."		

Great, you should now have a better understanding and feeling about your entrepreneurial self.

Let's now look at what life is really like as an entrepreneur. It's actually really great fun as well as hard work!

What have you learned:

Jane's learnings:

Basically I am good at putting things into action and communicating to people. I am quite persistent too but I need to think about any fears I have about trying new things and see how I can address that — I think adaptability and courage are connected for me. As far as vision is concerned — I know I don't immediately see how I would like things to turn out but as Mark says — I can do it when I have some great people to bounce ideas off. I actually feel like I'm already improving my ability to visualize using this process.

Mentor Session 3

Entrepreneurial Lifestyle

- What's life like as an entrepreneur?
- Ten great things about being an entrepreneur
- A story of entrepreneurial beginnings
- Lessons

What's life like as an entrepreneur?

In today's session I want to share the good, the bad and the ugly of life as an entrepreneur. While I want you to go into it with your eyes open I also want you to be encouraged by some of the great things about being an entrepreneur. I'll then share an inspiring story from one of my mentees to start igniting any potential entrepreneurial sparks.

Starting a business as a first time entrepreneur is one of those huge, life-altering events. It's actually a lot like a marriage – running a successful business takes just the same depth of commitment and desire. Like any relationship, if you want your business to be successful, you're going to have to work at it.

And if you are not married, let me tell you it means you're in for a roller-coaster ride of ups and downs and surprises!

Are you prepared for the emotional roller-coaster?

'Either way, it's fun, traumatic, hard work and incredibly rewarding all at once . . .'

Who wants to inflict that kind of trauma on themselves? Who wants to expose themselves to that kind of risk? Who wants to throw every ounce of themselves into what may be a futile effort, especially when conventional businesses offer plenty of jobs?

Being an entrepreneur has its ups and downs, often to the extreme of each. If you can turn your stumbling blocks into stepping stones then you are halfway to becoming a successful entrepreneur. A lot of start-up business books emphasize the mechanics of entrepreneurship: raising the money, finding an idea, and marketing the idea. Sure, there are basic steps to learn, but before you worry about mechanics, you should steel yourself for the emotional ups and downs that are inherent in the start-up world.

'More than half of all businesses that start up fail'

You've probably heard this statement – and my advice? Just ignore it!

This may seem odd, but in reality if you were frightened by a mere statistic you wouldn't be able to do all the other things required to make it as an entrepreneur. About half of all marriages fail, too, but that doesn't stop people from getting married, or from trying again after one marriage fails.

If you go into a business or a marriage thinking that you'll fail because most people do, chances are you will fail. It's that self-fulfilling prophecy thing. On the positive side, if you've got the right frame of mind and a solid plan, starting your own business can be the most satisfying and exhilarating experience of your life.

Long hours, no guaranteed salary

When you work for somebody, you generally know what's expected of you. You have a contract, or there are posted rules or a manual that tells you what you're expected to do and what your responsibilities are. You know what you'll be paid in exchange for doing those things, and you know there are limits as to where you can go in the job.

When you work for yourself, the expectations are generally less clear-cut than they are when you work for somebody else. An entrepreneur's guideline for hours and salary would look something like this:

- Hours? Until the work is done.
- Salary? Whatever the business can afford after everyone else is paid.

In addition to working long hours, you're going to have to work the jobs of more than one person. You're likely to be a worker, a manager, a secretary, a coach, a salesperson, a marketer, an accountant and anything else that is required to meet the ultimate goal when you don't have the resources to hire someone to do it for you.

> **INSIDER TIP**
>
> In case you think there is a short cut to this one, forget it!
>
> Long hours seem to be a universal requirement of any early stage business so don't get started unless you and your family can handle the implications.

It can be lonely at the top

You also need to be aware that many new entrepreneurs find it very lonely being a new boss, even if they've headed up a corporate business before. People often underestimate how much they relied on having people around them or the importance of chats around the water cooler. There are often few opportunities to connect to people like this on a daily basis. You will need to make new friends and find new ways to connect. Fortunately there is probably a networking group in your town, but it means making a special effort to find people to spend time with.

Ten great things about being an entrepreneur

Now for the positive stuff! We have covered some of the more challenging areas, but of course if it was all bad no one would do it. For most of us the great things far outweigh the bad; here are just a small number of those positive examples:

1 You make the rules now

Yes, it's up to you; you make the decisions on your life and the direction of your business. No more having to wait for approvals or missing opportunity. No more getting frustrated at others' poor decisions or bad behaviour – you get to decide!

2 It's your baby

Not only do you make the rules but you have the fun of naming your baby, and deciding its future from the logo to the mission statement. You can plot your own path safe in the knowledge that you stand or fall on your own merits. If you put in the effort you get a direct reward for it. You even get to have your name across the door and to stamp your own personality across the business.

3 No more politics

No, you don't have to get in at 7 a.m. or leave your jacket on your chair all night any more, just to impress or compete with colleagues. You come to work when you want, it's up to you, you don't need to clock watch anymore.

4 Time flexibility

You can choose your hours and work when you need to. If your business idea means you can play golf every day, spend time with the kids or work to your personal body clock, then that's what you do. No more having to stick to the 9 'til 5. Go on as many holidays as you can afford or have time for.

5 Work where you want

No more need to commute to work. If you want to work from home, or set up an office around the corner and ride your bike to work, you can do it. No more wasted time and stress on the road if you don't want to. One friend of mine relocated to the British Virgin Islands just because he liked the weather – how's that for choice!

6 Work with who you want

No more having to work with a low quality team or difficult people. Employ those you respect and enjoy working with. If you don't gel with an employee, then cut them loose. The same applies to your customers and suppliers. In my business we have a culture based on 'fun, service and profit'. This means we only work with colleagues, suppliers and customers who are fun and contribute 150% to each other – that's how we make profit! If they don't fit we don't do business.

7 Run your life how you want to

If you want to work in a particular style then you can. Work at 2 a.m. and go home at 3 p.m., great. You can mix holidays with business travel without anyone saying 'no you can't'. You get to mould the corporate culture just as you want. If you want a cool, chilled-out office with sofas rather than a subdued white-walled corporate environment, then you can.

8 Leverage your dreams and imagination

Follow your own ideas and have the freedom to change them whenever you want. If everyone else says it's a crazy idea but you believe in it, that's your choice. If you have an idea about a new way to structure your relationships with staff or customers, just do it. Even if you want to try a collection of different ideas at once – go ahead!

9 Money flexibility

This cuts both ways. Often it's tough to start, but once you are successful you get to choose the very lowest tax options. You can invest your money how you want and get some great pension and investment options not always open to employees. You can use your profits how you decide, from buying other businesses to taking nice fat dividends. You could assist a local charity or buy a second home. It's up to you.

10 A sense of pride and satisfaction

Of course, one of the great rewards of running your own venture is that all the successes (and failures) are your own to claim. When you win a contract, or a new client, or an award, it's all down to you – so well done! You can get the acclaim and genuine respect of your friends and family.

The story of an entrepreneurial beginning

Bringing together some of the things we have spoken about in this session, a former mentee of mine from the London Business School, Peter Ward, is going to share with you his inspiring story about setting out on his own path and eventually creating one of Europe's most successful internet companies:

An entrepreneurial beginning

'I have a passion for new ideas and seeing them come to life. Ever since I was a kid, I would get such a sense of joy when an idea, often in collaboration with others, would get everyone involved excited and motivated to work hard as part of a team.

'My first recollection of this was when I suggested to three of my school friends in primary school, (when I was about 8 or 9) that we write a book based on Jules Verne's *Around the World in 80 Days* about the adventures of Phileas Fogg. As a team, the four of us imagined the departing from Bombay (Mumbai) on a train and travelling across the Indian subcontinent into South East Asia and beyond. We wrote over 150 pages in a matter or weeks, and we were rewarded by having the teacher read it to the entire class as the daytime story.

'Since then, I was always enchanted by travel and following through with new ideas. My next major project at school when I was about 13, and me and a friend decided to set up a video club for students, so that students could watch movies after school hours. By selling fun-sized chocolates and cups of soft drinks, we managed to raise enough money to buy a top-of-the-range computer for the school.

'Whilst at university, despite believing that one day I would become an entrepreneur, I found myself becoming more influenced by the idea of working for a large and credible corporate company, such as a management consultancy or investment bank. This was, in part, I think, because the careers counselling did very little to promote entrepreneurship as a career choice.

'Hungry for success in my first year of university, I differentiated myself by becoming actively involved in other activities over and above study, which would help me prepare for a career after university. So I decided to work with a small team of students to launch the SIS Skills Society at Brunel University. As 'Events Coordinator', I helped organize as many as four to five events per week with leading companies. The whole point of the society and my involvement with them was to develop the relevant skills and contacts in order to prepare myself for work after graduating.

'I was fortunate enough to attend a talk with a leading entrepreneur named Marcus Orlovski, who set up a property development company having discussed the idea with his pals in a wine bar. In a very short space of time, they managed to bring on board a leading UK law firm and an American architect, to put together a proposal for the redevelopment of Liverpool Street Station, known as 'Bishopsgate and Broadgate'. They successfully convinced relevant stakeholders that this derelict piece of land in the centre of London re-presented a great leasing potential for leading internal investment. They were eventually oversubscribed with Japanese, American and European banks and managed to generate over £250 million from the project. This one talk reawakened the entrepreneurial spirit in me and reminded me that anything is possible.

'From that point on, I maintained an entrepreneurial viewpoint in the back of my mind, and went about trying out different business ideas whilst at university. These included organizing parties for the students union, and creating a company to use interactive party games to break down social barriers between people. I then set up a new society called eBiz Networks, with the aim of bringing together like-minded people who had an interest in entrepreneurship and the new internet and e-business revolution. It was as a result of this that I, along with some of our members, was invited to attend the entrepreneurship summer school at Cambridge University on a fellowship. I felt very privileged and motivated by my involvement in a programme designed to equip me with the skills to become a successful entrepreneur from such a reputable educational institution. My business idea at the time, which was to launch a career development and graduate recruitment company, reached the finals of the Cambridge Enterprise Business Plan competitions, which was a huge vote of confidence in me and my idea.

'To hone my skills, I then applied to attend the London Business School Entrepreneurship Programme, which at £9K a pop, was a significant investment. I managed to get a fellowship from London Business School to meet half the costs and borrowed the rest of the money from my parents. This gave me the opportunity to further test out my current business idea, having recently come back from 9 months of travelling around the world since my last entrepreneurship programme.

'It was at this time that I received a phone call from my friend, who I was about to start work with at Accenture, who told me of his idea to visualize his contacts on a world map, which would eventually become WAYN.com, the world's largest travel and lifestyle social network. I immediately took to the idea and decided not to pursue the career management and recruitment initiative and instead, took a job offer from Accenture. I had racked up over £30K of debt from university, travelling and paying for training courses, and it seemed the sensible thing to do. It would also allow me to work on WAYN as it was not something that would require time during the day to work on. Instead, we worked on it in our spare time from our back bedrooms, on weekends and late evenings after long days at the Accenture office (which is not exactly 9 to 5!).

'I then managed to get Accenture to sponsor me for entrepreneurship training at the Sloan School of Business at MIT in Boston, MA, USA, where they met half of the $13K costs and all travel-related expenses, and the Cambridge and MIT Institute met the other half of the fees. This provided me with international connections and a chance to further develop my entrepreneurial skills.

'I finally managed to realize my dream of becoming a fully fledged entrepreneur in October 2005 when I took a leave of absence from Accenture to work on WAYN full time. It was a smooth and pragmatic transition as WAYN had already started to take off in March 2005, having grown from 45,000 members to over 1 million members, and this meant we were able to pay ourselves the equivalent of our salary at Accenture. I also had the added comfort of a 6–12 month sabbatical, which meant that if the business didn't take off, I had a safety net with a reputable firm to work for.

'Since then, we have grown WAYN to become the world's largest travel and lifestyle social network, with over 9 million members and over 4 million unique visitors returning to the site every month. We raised $11M Venture capital funding in November 2006 and secured a leading team of advisers including Brent Hoberman, co-founder and former CEO of lastminute.com, which was sold to Travelocity for over $1billion. Right now, we have a team of over 40 staff in two locations, and are working hard to improve the product, increase growth and establish ourselves as a leading travel portal. Wish us luck . . .'

Peter Ward, *Co-CEO, WAYN*

Lessons

Why not spend some time reflecting on what you think the life an entrepreneur could be like for you? What are the possibilities? What (if anything yet!) motivates you about the lifestyle?

Consider Peter's story. Imagine what your success story will read like, what will you be known for? What will you have achieved?

Being an entrepreneur means the following to me:

Jane:

Hmm . . . real life as an entrepreneur! I guess I had a vague idea about the fact that it is an emotional rollercoaster but I always thought of this as a negative. Suddenly, I am actually finding it quite a motivating point — it sounds exciting. I know I have to work on adaptability and I am not underestimating how difficult this would be, but when I read through the good points about being an entrepreneur it seems to address all the things I have issue or concern with right now.

I really loathe to follow someone else's rules, not all of them, just that ones that don't make sense to me or impede progress or creativity. I find it so frustrating. I hate the politics that I have to deal with on a daily basis, the stuff that makes people too afraid to question or propose a new way of doing something.

I would love to have a job where I could dictate the hours and nature of my day — not that I am lazy — quite the opposite in fact . . . It's just a nine to five job feels so restrictive. Being able to pick the hours, the people and the location of work sounds like a dream doesn't it? Could this be my dream? So, assuming I could do anything, what could I do?

- Baby food company
- Organic catering company
- Karaoke-catered parties (with equipment?)
- Go and work for the competition for a better salary and a gas guzzling company car

What would my story sound like?

2 years ago I started my nationwide baby food company, how far I've come since then . . .

2 years ago I started my organic catering company, we now have over 20 people in 3 different locations across the region . . .

2 years ago I started my own catered Karaoke party company . . .

2 years ago I went against all my better instincts and sold my soul to the competition for a better pay and a revolting status car which goes against all my principles . . .

Let's see what the next session brings . . . I think I know how I would like my story to play out but I will hold off.

Hopefully you are getting a bit more excited now? Can you see yourself overcoming the hurdles and enjoying the benefits of being an entrepreneur now? Let's get into the detail behind you now, read on to uncover your hidden skills and talents.

INSIDER TIP

Another incredibly powerful tool you can learn is "visualisation".

This is the ability to imagine our future in bright and colorful images: the nice house, happy smiling people that you have helped or anything else you want in your life. Take the time learn more about this in your own time if you want to get massive leverage on your dreams.

Mentor Session 4

Deconstructing You – Part 1

- Taking a personal inventory and assessing your current resources
- Audit your business history and abilities
- Management skills evaluation
- Personality evaluation
- Lessons

Welcome to the fourth mentoring session. At this stage you probably have a really good feel for entrepreneurial life and the highs and lows involved. If you have been relating the information back to your own circumstances, and following the exercises as you go along, then you probably already have a good idea of how suited you are to an entrepreneurial profession. This session is designed to take it down to the next level of detail, and really examine you and the resources available to you to make a success of this. You will find it a lot more hands-on, so pen to the ready!

Taking a personal inventory and assessing your current resources

We are now going go much deeper into you and what you bring to the table. The simplest and easiest way to do this is to carry out a personal inventory and that's what we're going to do now. You will be amazed at the resources and connections you actually have, and they could eventually make a big difference to the outcome of your business. This in itself can be really exciting and motivational. Try and make this as comprehensive as you can, even if you feel it's a drag having to do it – and to be fair, many entrepreneurs hate paperwork.

New entrepreneurs often underestimate what they will need to start their businesses. As we know, anyone can start a company, but we also know that only a small percentage of those attempting it actually succeed. In one way or another, the reasons for failure come down to 'resources', both personal and material. The businesses that fail, most often do so because they lack money (or financial know-how), industry expertise, or a viable strategic plan.

Let's get started by completing a thorough, honest appraisal of you and your personal commitments together with your business needs and goals. We will focus on your strong points, identify your weaknesses, and deal with areas that need improvement. Most people have never completed this type of exercise. *As a result you will have a much better chance of success from the outset.*

Experience tells us that entrepreneurs have all sorts of different characters and abilities. Anyone can start a business and potentially achieve success, from the painfully shy Michael Dell (Dell), to Alan Sugar (Amstrad) without a formal education, the enigmatic Steve Jobs (Apple) or the outspoken like Oracle's Larry Ellison. But one thing that every successful entrepreneur will have to do is to manage counterproductive characteristics, and supplement missing capabilities, underdeveloped skills and psychological attitudes that could create roadblocks to their eventual success. They look for help from team members to make up for any shortcomings.

Some people don't want to acknowledge their inadequacies, but those that do will be massively increasing the chances of success. If the potential entrepreneur prefers not to face his human limitations, he might be better off staying in a traditional job.

I know that's not going to be you, so let's move on. It is important to be free from distractions to obtain the best results. If like me, you usually struggle a bit with these things, have a few goes at it until you feel you have uncovered everything as far as you can. You can also revisit it later as other ideas and people come into your head.

Audit your business history and abilities

One of other key things we know is that many entrepreneurs leave their jobs out of frustration, but stay in the same field and start a competing business or just develop an idea their company didn't want to explore. In any case, the skills and resources you have gleaned from any work experience will probably be very important in your new business; indeed, they may be critical. So the first step is to explore in depth your work history.

INSIDER TIP

Many investors prefer funding entrepreneurs who show strong subject matter experience. Try and find a link between what you know and your business dream.

Autobiography

Dig out your résumé/curriculum vitae if you have one, and use this information to write a summary of your own biography. Review in detail all the facets of your past, including work positions, projects you have done, education, credentials you have earned, family and personal relationships.

Include all your work experiences during summers, weekends or holidays. As with a regular CV, start with your current achievements and work backwards.

List all the roles you have assumed in your present or past jobs in order of importance (e.g. responsibility, authority, budgeting, selling).

Try and find matches between your past and your idea. How will your expertise in, say, 'accounts' help you start a business? What have you learned that has either general or specific use in the idea or venture?

My autobiography

Your notes:

This will be a longer answer so either copy the heading onto your notebook or download the forms from the site: www.tobeanentrepreneur.com.

Jane's notes:

Catering company logistics manager

- Assessing customer needs
- Optimizing customer delivery schedule
- Sourcing and managing suppliers
- Managing fleet of delivery vans
- Budget

Projects —
Introducing organic and fair trade options
Introduction of quarterly payment options for schools
Catering company logistics assistant manager
Documenting customer needs
Resolving customer complaints

-Award for 'employee with most innovative idea'
-Best practice award
Staff Christmas party management
Staff summer BBQ management
School canteen student monitor

Helped create new breads that became the top sellers of the summer.

Supporting manager with suppliers *School —* *High school Baccalaureate* *Work experience —* *6 weeks travel company* *Summer job in bakery*	

At this point you may be wondering why we bother to fill out all these forms – good question. They are designed to help you either start a process of finding the best idea to suit you, or to find out if the idea you already have in mind will be a good fit or not. Hang in there, effort put in at this time will pay dividends.

How do you see these *job role areas* assisting you in your business goals?

Job role areas

Your notes:

This will be a longer answer so either copy the heading onto your notebook or download the forms from the site: www.tobeanentrepreneur.com.

Jane's notes:

Looking at my list from the last session

Baby food company — Organic catering company

Karaoke-catered parties (with equipment)

Go and work for the competition for a better salary and a gas guzzling company car

Probably the organic catering company is the one that jumps out at me, my jobs to date (my two!) mean that I have a good grounding in all the relevant areas. Even as a catering logistics assistant, I had to listen to so many complaints I am an expert on how 'not to' do things.

I think I really want to stay in the catering world and maybe set up my own niche catering business. My company just doesn't see the value in following the trend for home grown, organic produce cooked well — it's too expensive apparently. I think it's about finding a balance. People will pay for quality and I know how to source some great suppliers. Maybe I have more vision than I give myself credit for!

Hint

Don't forget you can download these forms: www .tobeanentrepreneur.com

Knowledge

What do you *know* about the business or idea you plan to start? List all the things *you know* about the business or idea in as much detail as you can. This will help create a checklist for more research or information.

Do your homework before you jump in. Even before I write a business plan I now do months of research in as much depth as I can. For example, with one idea I travelled to the UK, USA and Australia visiting hair salons and making notes. Then I worked in one for a while, simply observing before going on a relevant training course and spending lots of time with friends that owned salons . . . all to understand the business before deciding to invest my time and money!

Try and find matches between your knowledge and direct experience and your idea. If you know about building aeroplanes and you think you have found a cheaper way to make them, explain why here.

How do you see your *knowledge* assisting you in your business goals?

Knowledge

Your notes:

This will be a longer answer so either copy the heading onto your notebook or download the forms from the site: www.tobeanentrepreneur.com.

Jane's notes:

OK, so, if I was to follow the organic catering company idea. How would my knowledge best support this . . . well, I know what customers want these days because I'm the only one that bothers to go and sit and talk with them. I lead a project around the cost benefit analysis of providing organic produce, ethically grown and I gained a lot of knowledge in doing this (despite the fact that my own company rejected the idea).

I know the difficulties involved with distribution but I have some great ideas for that. I have the data on costs of home grown organic versus the alternative and customer price tolerance levels. If my thinking is right I can really make it work. I have friends who work from home who never have time to make nutritious meals, maybe I could focus on them and the incapacitated to start with before I try and hit the small businesses — the ones that can't afford in-house catering for staff. I do have lists of names and numbers and great relationships with a lot of them!

The question is 'Have I got what it takes to actually "run" my own business?' Hopefully the management skills evaluation we do next will help me.

Management skills evaluation

Now let's look at core strengths and weaknesses with regard to *executing* your vision.

Again, this exercise is sharpening your personal awareness about areas for improvement, or where you need other team members to supplement your skills. This is a great way to get a team together, because you will be able to highlight what you like and want to do and things you wish to delegate to others who have their strengths in those areas – this empowers your team, and again improves your chances of long term success.

Choose your skill level from 1–3, and remember this relates to your goal, or business or idea, and not life in general. How developed is your skill-set towards achieving your specific business opportunity? Remember to be totally honest with yourself.

1. No ability in this area or a major weakness – must delegate.
2. Average ability, but could improve or delegate.
3. Proven ability in this area.

This list is not exhaustive, and you can add to it on your own – especially if you have a clear business idea in mind. It's aimed at a start-up business and is designed to stimulate debate rather than ask every possible question of your abilities. Some of these skills will not be relevant and some will be missing; update where necessary. Don't worry about ignoring ones that don't seem useful – just mark those 'not applicable'.

General management skills	*Your answers*	*Jane's answers*
Communications		3
Law (corporate/contract/ tax/patent/hr)		1
Networking		2
Public speaking		2
Due diligence		3
Planning		3
Project management		3
Purchasing		3
Business systems and processes		2
Technical skills		
Research		3
Development		3

Project management	*3*
Manufacturing or product production	*2*
Service development and management	*3*
Technical expertise in business or field	*3*
Engineering management	*Not applicable*
Patent and intellectual property (IP) protection	*1*
Quality control systems	*3*

Sales skills

Sales experience and sales management	*2*
Sales systems implementation	*2*
Sales training	*2*
Pitching	*1*
Major account management	*2*
Channel development	*Not applicable*
USP and customer value development	*3*

Marketing skills

Market evaluation and research	*3*
Media buying and management	*1*
Market segmentation	*2*

Materials development	1
Go to market strategy development	1
Branding strategy	2
E-marketing expertise	1
Agency selection, management and control	1
Events management	2

Financial skills

Business plan writing	2
Financial modelling	2
Understanding or experience of fund raising	1
Money management and control	2
Financial systems	2
Credit planning and cash collection	2
Purchasing	3
Working with banks, angels, venture capitalists and other finance sources	1
Tax, HR, R&D and other cost planning	3

Operational skills

Office management and admin skills	2

Setup and establishment of offices, factories or outlets	3
Manufacturing, development or service organization management	3
Production and inventory control	3
HR and related people systems	1
IT, telephony and other systems management	1
Customer service	3
Quality assurance	3
Legal and government regulations	2
Insurance and other business protection planning	1

People skills

Recruitment and interviewing	2
Company 'culture' development	2
Payroll and management systems	1
Staff motivation and communication	3
Staff training and development	2
Staff incentives, options and rewards	2
Staff events	3

Overview of results

Now give yourself a quick rating on your specific skills.

Strengths	Average – improve or delegate	Poor – delegate
Yours:		
Jane's:		
Communication	Financial	Systems of all kinds
Planning & project management.	People skills esp. payroll systems etc Sales	Working with banks & VCs
Customer service		Law
Quality assurance Purchasing		Marketing

Notes:

Note here any thoughts on how you could improve, team members or friends with skills you need, outsourcing or other ways to fill any skill gaps.

Try and identify specific people and skills if you can along with who you could see yourself working with as the "team" for your new venture.

Useful skills and people I need:

Jane's:

Assuming I developed a type of catering company, based on organic principles, how would my management evaluation tie in? My main skill gap is any IT/systems areas but I am hoping there won't be much of that. I don't have any marketing experience but I have loads of school friends that went into marketing, I could look for advice from them — maybe some of them would even be interested in joining forces if my idea sounds like a flyer. Law and IP stuff is really out of my league, but if it wasn't I'd be a lawyer right?!

INSIDER TIP

One of the greatest strengths of successful people is the ability to get things done. This usually means understanding what you are good at and delegating the rest.

Don't think you have to do it all, make sure you are clear on how you can add maximum value and then find others to help with everything else.

Personality evaluation

OK, now let's consider a bit more about our own lives and our personality. This exercise is useful for understanding how we work with others, but also once again in choosing a business that will suit us.

In this exercise, think about who you really are. Don't try and make something up that's not totally honest; this is for your eyes only!

Consider your responses in various situations and in working with others; choose from the options below, or make up your own. Remember, this is only designed to help you decide on how to plan your business, or perhaps your best role in the start-up team. There are no right or wrong answers. You will react differently in different situations, so apply this to a work situation.

In my case I find that I am more reserved, dominant; a little shy, driven, self-assured and objective. So my personal work from this process is to try and be better at working with people. I try harder to overcome the shy and reserved part of my personality when running my businesses – what would you work on? Having seen the attributes of successful entrepreneurs you can see that being shy isn't ideal as you have to get out there and sell yourself, your business and to meet many people! Being shy hasn't stopped me, and your personality shouldn't stop you.

Put a circle around one or more in each category (Jane's are underlined):

Response to people
Warm, outgoing, <u>attentive to others,</u> kindly, easygoing, <u>participating</u>, likes people, cool, reserved, impersonal, detached.

Dominance
Dominant, forceful, assertive, aggressive, competitive, <u>stubborn</u>, bossy, deferential, cooperative, avoids conflict, submissive, humble, obedient, easily led.

Socially
Socially bold, venturesome, <u>thick-skinned</u>, uninhibited, shy, timid, hesitant.

Self-reliance
Self-reliant, solitary, resourceful, <u>individualistic</u>, self-sufficient, group-oriented, a joiner and follower dependent.

Openness to change
Experimental, liberal, analytical, critical, free thinking, traditional, <u>attached to familiar</u>, <u>conservative</u>, respecting traditional ideas.

Drive level
Tense, <u>high energy</u>, impatient, driven, frustrated, relaxed patient, placid, tranquil, torpid.

Confidence
Self-assured, unworried, <u>confident</u>, self-satisfied, apprehensive, self-doubting, worried, guilt-prone, insecure, worrying, self-blaming.

Sensitivity
<u>Objective</u>, unsentimental, tough-minded, <u>self-reliant</u>, no-nonsense, sensitive, aesthetic, sentimental, tender-minded, intuitive.

Dependability
Empowered, caring, dependable, <u>trusting</u>, honest, truthful, uncaring, confrontational, unreliable, suspicious, dishonest.

Fairness
<u>Appreciative</u>, impartial, <u>tolerant</u>, ungrateful, biased, intolerant.

> **INSIDER TIP**
>
> Have you ever done any work or school-related personality tests? These can be useful here, so dig any out and jot down what they say about you.

This quick process should make it clear to you what type of personality you are in the work situation. Are you an introvert or extrovert? This will help you decide if you are happy being the front man or woman, or whether you would rather manage things from a back seat. Are you assertive or passive – will you drive things or would you rather be a member of a team? Using these examples and the categories above, work through your personality profile and make notes on how this affects your view of your role in a start-up or for the life as an entrepreneur.

Personality category

Your notes:

Personality category

Jane's notes:

Response to people	*Attentive to others — this is good as I need to work closely with a number of people to make my business work.*

Dominance	Stubborn — this can be good if people are trying to put me off starting my business but I had better be careful how it affects my working with colleagues.
Socially	Thick-skinned — again, great for the life as an entrepreneur.
Self-reliance	Individualistic — again, great for the life as an entrepreneur.
Openness to change	Attached — I see that action and change are all part of the daily life of an entrepreneur so I need to loosen up a bit here.
Drive level	Impatient — can be a double-edged sword.
Confidence	Confident — excellent, definitely in top 10 traits.
Sensitivity	Self-reliant — again really good.
Dependability	Trusting — as long as I keep this in check I think it will help rather than hinder me.
Fairness	Tolerant — I am bound to come into contact with people from all walks of life as an entrepreneur so this will be really important.

(Adapted from Cattell's Sixteen Personality Factor Model)

> **INSIDER TIP**
>
> It should be obvious that the more we understand "ourselves" the better and then it makes it easier to let others know how we like to work and also we get a greater sense about others and the best way we can motivate and lead them.
>
> Don't be afraid to face up to your shortcomings, it will make you stronger and more likely to succeed. No-one is perfect!

Accomplishments

List your accomplishments. Try and be specific and pull from memory relevant things that you think are useful, fun or important. Anything goes – did you win a prize as a kid, or did you contribute to helping people, help someone cross the road, raise funds for charity, captain the football team, write a great piece of work, paint, sing, or whatever! Whatever comes to mind that made you think, 'I loved doing that'?

At work, did you win employee of the month, get a compliment from management or a customer, win a sales or customer service award, organize or contribute to something special, sell to a big client . . . whatever comes to mind!

Non-job-related accomplishments

Jane's:

Community 'Meals on Wheels' for the old and infirm — volunteer for most of teenage years.

Children's party planner for a few summers to make some money as a teenager.

Started residents' committee in flats I am living in.

Work-related accomplishments

Jane's:

Led project to assess the viability of including a fully organic range into the catering line.

Coordination of staff social events — summer BBQ & Christmas party.

Won employee 'Best Practice' award.

Won 'most innovative idea' award for new payment option for schools.

Successfully introduced a quarterly payment option for schools.

Review the accomplishments and observe your talents

The exercise above is trying to highlight what you are good at from both a work and social point of view. It also points to things that you *enjoy* and could potentially develop into a business skill or long term asset. These are important, compared with skills you have had to learn, as they tend to be things you have a *special talent* for that you may not have really noticed before. These talents will help you focus yourself on what's best for you.

Accomplishment	Skills used to achieve it	What talent does this display?
Yours:		

Accomplishment	Skills used to achieve it	What talent does this display?
Jane's:		
'Meals on Wheels' volunteer	Assessing needs Coordinating & Planning meals Coordinating delivery rounds Budgeting	understanding of varying needs of customers Ability to coordinate full sweep of catering considerations Ability to work to a tight budget.

Kids' Party Planner	Creative ideas Coordinating several parties at once	Ability to think 'outside the box' Ability to multi task
Work summer BBQ & Christmas parties	Work to budget Coordinate entertainment & food suppliers Manage advertising print and distribution	Ability to work to a tight budget Ability to develop creative ideas understanding of print promotion
Payment option for schools	Liaise with key staff at school Brainstorm ideas to allow them to make the most of their quarterly budget	Ability to interact with staff and management at all levels Ability to generate creative ideas
Project to assess the viability of an organic line	Analyze suppliers Assess market appetite Perform cost projections	understanding of market understanding of suppliers' strengths and weaknesses

INSIDER TIP

Don't hide your talents, be fully aware of them, this is not about bragging rights it's about helping shape your future.

Everyone in the world has a special talent and the sooner you find yours the better. Once you are clear about it then the sooner you can start to use it to propel you towards your dreams.

Your health position

Now let's look at the physical factors. In order to take on a start-up or life as an entrepreneur, you will be exposing yourself to extremes of everything from stress to loneliness, from long days to lots of frustration. It's important you are aware of your overall health and mental stamina.

General health

Is it good? Are you prone to illness? How do you cope with stress? Do you have high blood pressure or any other health issues you should consider?

Physical stamina

Can you work long hours without sleep? Do you have a lot of energy and can you sustain your concentration in tough situations? Does your idea require lots of stamina?

Physical exertion

Be honest – are you a lazy type physically or do you struggle to sit down? Are you generally fit and using exercise regularly? Do you prefer to be outside or inside?

Mental strength

Can you relax easily? How do you cope under pressure? How do you cope with having to make lots of decisions at once, sometimes without much supporting information? What's your propensity for risk and how do you cope when you make a mistake?

In considering these factors you should not only think about your role but also the type of business you think you might want to start. It's no good being a couch potato and hating exercise if you want to market a health product, for example. You may laugh, but I have seen issues like this come up again and again. There needs to be a good fit between your health and the business you are planning.

INSIDER TIP

Don't join the many entrepreneurs that sacrifice their health for their business.

Be clear from the get go what you are capable of and what you want from life as far as your health is concerned and make sure your business delivers on that, not the other way round.

How do you see your *physical profile* assisting you in your business goals?

Make more notes in the downloaded sheets, see Jane's note for any guidance.

Physical profile

Your notes:

This will be a longer answer so either copy the heading onto your notebook or download the forms from the site: www.tobeanentrepreneur.com.

Jane's:

I think at this stage I am homing in on an organic home delivery/catering company. This is not a million miles away from what I do now and I love being out and about going from supplier to supplier and visiting customers. I don't think I would like to be stuck in an office all day, but if I launch the healthy lunches (. . . just thought, we can market the diet lunches thing) for home workers or small businesses then it would be just me doing the prep and delivery etc. so I think I should be OK.

> I have a lot of energy usually but I do get stress-related migraine — mostly brought on by my boss, so maybe they will be a thing of the past?! Children's party planner for a few summers to make some money as a teenager.
>
> Started residents' committee in flats I am living in.

What interests you in life?

In this section we need to list your hobbies, activities, the times you are most happy or joyful. What do get passionate about? Sports or books? Working inside an office or outside in the sunshine? What do you wish you could do or would do *with no limits*?

In the previous section I stressed the importance of matching your lifestyle and interests to your idea. A great example of this issue is a former mentee, who had a big plan for a software start-up; it was a good idea and really had possibilities. However, there were a few big issues when he brought the plan to me. The first questions I asked were those in this book, and to cut a long story short, he was a former champion skier, loved car racing, running and being outdoors! *He wanted an active lifestyle and to be out of the office.*

How do you think this squared with his plan for a new business? It was totally wrong, and after we completed these exercises he realized he didn't want the life of a software start-up, i.e. in the office on a PC eighteen hours a day in a cube! He also didn't really like the risks and time commitment away from his important sports and hobbies. In the end he decided to take a job with a big consulting company and *this was the right decision for him.*

Recreational activities/hobbies

List the recreational activities in which you participate in order of importance, (e.g. hiking, jogging, tennis, skiing, sailing, cycling, skating, exercise classes, dancing, reading, flying a kite, computer gaming, travel, eating and drinking, singing, yoga . . .).

Favourite activities/hobbies

Jane's:

Eating with friends.
Cooking for anyone who will eat my food!
Reading about the origins of food products.
Singing — karaoke!
Mountain biking
Tennis (badly)
Yoga (reluctantly)

How do you see these areas of *activity* assisting you in your business goals?

Activities

Your notes:

This will be a longer answer so either copy the heading onto your notebook or download the forms from the site: www.tobeanentrepreneur.com.

Jane's:

I feel better and better about my business ideas as it will mix a lot of what I do outside work. Thinking about how much I love being on the bike . . . maybe I could even have delivery on a fleet of bicycles — eco-friendly lunches. Even better! The karaoke I might need to keep as a hobby, I might enjoy it but no one else seems to enjoy it very much!

Don't worry if your hobbies have nothing to do with your idea or you don't have a relevant hobby. This whole process is meant to be simple and fun. If you don't have a fit here, just skip the section and move on. If you can do it though, it's worth it as sometimes you find that your original business idea isn't the right fit for you; and this process can make you think of new and interesting business possibilities.

INSIDER TIP

We can't all have businesses related directly to our hobbies but thinking about them can really help you understand your own motivations and needs.

Also, while we may not be actively doing a hobby orientated business we may wish to start a business that enables us to engage in the things we love to do more than now - your business needs to serve you and give you the best in life including doing the things you love to do.

Love what you do, do what you love . . .

So why did I get you to look at your hobbies and favourite pastimes? If you end up choosing a business that is closely related to *what you love and enjoy doing*, then you have a great chance of success. Many strive for this goal, but it's a lot more complex than the words allow us to believe.

The core message is sound, however, and one of the greatest things about being an entrepreneur, in all its many guises, is that we are more likely than any other group to achieve this.

If you have taken the concepts in this book to heart and you now know what it is you want out of life and what you think you want to do that gives you that 'fire' in your belly, then the life of an entrepreneur will be something you just love doing.

Don't get me wrong; it's like anything else in that some days are better than others, but there is a reason why so many people leave a safe job and never go back – they find their passion and do what they love by doing their own thing.

Roper Starch polled the founders of *INC.* magazine's 500 fastest growing firms in America between 1992 and 1996 and compared their responses with 200 high-level executives of *Fortune* 500 companies.

Among the survey's conclusions:

69% of the entrepreneurs, but only 40% of the executives, agreed with the statement 'I love what I do for a living.'

Asked what would they do if they could live their lives over, more than one-third of the corporate executives said they would choose to run their own company.

So what do you love then, what is your passion? You should have a good idea by now. Do you think you can express it in a simple statement now? Have a try. . .

If I could do what I love, my business would be:

What about your family and network?

In this context, what we are trying to discover is the extent of your 'people' connections. Do you have any role models, and people you can bounce ideas off, people who will provide expertise, experience, money, support or contacts? We should list as many of these people that are relevant, and we will try and organize them in areas of usefulness.

This is a really important section as this is the most likely place where you will find *essential start-up resources* like money and help. Many people don't 'mine' their readily available resources, and that just makes their lives harder and their idea less likely to succeed. A huge number of businesses are founded on money from friends and families – so don't miss out.

Network

List all the people you know; friends, family, colleagues, old school chums etc. List the types of business they are involved in, where relevant. How do you view them and their self-employed roles? Have you talked to them about how they enjoy their business?

Name of person	Money	Exper-tise	Connec-tions	Support	Know-ledge
Yours:					

Name of person	Money	Exper-tise	Connec-tions	Support	Know-ledge
Jane's:					
Family friend — Edward Hynes	Not sure if I could ask for invest-ment	Catering equip-ment company	Lots of contacts in the trade	Would be very helpful	25 years in catering
School friend — Anna Combs	N/A	Product manager for an organic baby food company	Lots of contacts with organic and home grown suppliers		Very up to date with the latest and greatest in ethical farming etc.
Uncle George — elderly relative	Said he would invest if he likes my business idea!!	N/A	Has a lot of business angel contacts	Limited ongoing support	Used to own a venture capital Company

INSIDER TIP

Don't forget to add family and distant relatives. When I was a kid starting my first business my mother sat down with the family address book and we wrote a letter to whole bunch of long-lost relatives asking for help and money. Quite a few wrote back with ideas, concerns or advice. None with money, it should be noted!!

In considering those that own a business or have created a start-up, how do you see these *people and 'resources'* assisting you in your business goals?

Have you considered the ideal lifestyle for you?

This is another critical area. For a start, what are you going to try and achieve with your business? Is it your plan to have a nice little business that allows you to keep up your family time and hobbies? This is probably a lifestyle type of business or a micro business. If your ambitions are larger and perhaps you see a big company employing lots of people, then this will be a totally different proposition. If you have a big idea that you think will take off and grow, but requires lots funding, we have another, and different challenge.

The key here is whether you will decide to build a 'lifestyle business' or something on a more ambitious scale. If it's a lifestyle business (often these are family businesses) then you will have different issues of control, growth, scale, and so on. In a very general sense, lifestyle businesses tend to be smaller by virtue of the fact the owners want control, and are focused on different things from those faced by the person who wants to rule the world. The latter will probably have to give a lot more of their life to the job and take a great deal more risks with the attendant issues. Of course, if successful the rewards will match this life investment and risk.

There's nothing wrong with lifestyle businesses, and most small enterprises fit into this category.

So consider what you want from your business and your life – are you likely to want a lifestyle business or a more aggressively focused one?

At this stage you probably have at least one idea buzzing around your head. I want you to maintain that momentum, so I would like you to record your idea/ideas and then write your next five steps personal action plan. This can consist of any five things that will move you a little closer towards your business idea. If you are still filtering ideas at this stage, revisit the action plan after you have completed the next session.

Business idea/ideas (If applicable)

Jane's:

Organic catering company

Personal action plan (If applicable)

Jane's:

- Speak to Edward Hynes about the cost of catering equipment and run high level idea past him.
- Speak to uncle George about investing in business and his business angel contacts.
- Call old friends from school now working in marketing.
- Draw up preliminary costs.
- Assess price points and potential revenue.

You probably have a surprising amount of people and resources available to assist you, don't you? And maybe an idea that has been born from your passions or been crafted to meet these? Let's keep up the momentum and dig deeper into your life goals and 'wants'.

INSIDER TIP

Many people don't take the time to really dig deep into the 'gold mine' of contacts, connections, family, friends, old colleagues and related resources before they start.

This is a huge mistake and means you increase the risk of failure when with a little effort you can have an amazing free resource working to help you achieve your dreams.

Don't be shy or lazy, get the most out of all of your assets.

Deconstructing You–Part 2

- What's your personal motivation?
- A story about finding your personal mission
- Vision, purpose and a personal mission statement
- Identifying personal criteria fit for your business
- It's not all about the 'money'
- The 'I want' list
- Lessons

Now we have started to really examine who you are and what resources you have from a functional point of view; let's get deeper into your <u>motivations</u> and what attracts you to the idea of being an entrepreneur.

In order to achieve our overall goal in helping you decide if you want to be an entrepreneur, there are two things you have to know – <u>where you are and where you want to get to</u>. So far we have identified where you are – we have learned about entrepreneurship and inventoried your own abilities and skills. In order to discover where you want to get to, we need to understand your motivations. So let's look at 'why' you might want to become an entrepreneur.

Many younger people I hear talk about becoming entrepreneurs seem to focus heavily on the 'getting rich quick' rationale, and yet most entrepreneurs I know definitely don't do it for the money (alone). So the question remains – why do we do it? Surely it's not just for the fun of it or because we woke up one day with a great idea. When we analyse the bones of what being an entrepreneurship is about – it's about creating wealth.

For many of us, including me, entrepreneurship is a way to deliver a higher level of freedom from the corporate hamster wheel – a way to exert our own force on the world – in my case it's a compulsion that leads to wealth rather than a compulsion for wealth itself.

The path to riches comes from being outstanding at what you do, or following your passion and executing to such an extent that the riches come as if by magic. No one I know has ever become rich and stayed so for long by simply 'chasing the money'.

What's your personal motivation?

Why do <u>you</u> want to do start a business or become an entrepreneur? All reasons are valid, but once you have your reasons, you might want to explore whether there are other paths to reaching your goal.

Are you happy enough with a corporate life?

If so, will you be motivated enough to make it on your own? Or are you resigned to the corporate life? If not, why is that? Think about it, because maybe entrepreneurship will not give you what you are looking for either.

Imagine the destination, the final goal; your big dream . . . does it make you want to work as hard as you will have to?

Imagine the process, how to get there . . . will you be able to do it, motivate a team and have some fun along the way?

Imagine you fail . . . does the thought of failing motivate you to make it or have the opposite effect?

Identifying your reasons
Do the following reasons apply to you?

1. Being free from the nine-to-five daily work routine.
2. Being your own boss.
3. Doing what you want when you want to do it.
4. Improving your standard of living.
5. Escaping the boredom of your current job.
6. Selling a product or service for which you feel there is a demand.

List other reasons why you want to become an entrepreneur:

Reasons	Notes
Yours:	

Reasons	Notes
Jane's:	
Selling a product or service which I feel there is a demand for. Being my own boss. Allow me the freedom to pick and choose my hours and lifestyle.	Catering is a booming business. The busier we all become the more we 'outsource' all the different parts of our life. People assume people from home have lots of time to make nutritious healthy food — the fact is they often are too busy or trying to watch their weight so they don't keep lots of food in the house (is this relevant? Read up about diet plan — delivered calorie counted nutritious meals for the day to your door!? Small businesses usually require regular delivery or occasional catering as they do not have the resources to have an in-house catering facility.

Give yourself some time to let the ideas take root. In the meantime my friend Adam Miller has kindly agreed to relay his story. It serves as a reminder that sometimes the risk is worth the reward if your heart is really in it . . .

A story about finding your personal mission:

'I was eighteen and working for a 65-year-old carpenter in a family firm, making doors in a joiner's shop, when he one day reminded me that he had been doing the same job for over 50 years. I went home that night and wrote my resignation letter. All I knew was that I wanted to have a different life and one that I chose and controlled. I didn't have a clue what I was going to do, I just knew it wasn't that and I needed to earn money to survive.

'I started to valet cars, and went round all the car dealers in town trying to get work for my car valet business, and finally after visiting over 50 of them, someone gave me a car to clean. It was hard work, and I started to get more and more cars, and then was offered a full-time job by the garage. I thought about it for a few seconds but thanked them and said no. In the end, I tried about four or five things before I came across something that started to earn me money, where I wasn't working eighteen-hour days for minimum wage. As a serial entrepreneur, I always knew that the successes or failures were all mine and that I was in control of my life and my future and it felt great.

'I grew up in a very competitive family, played squash for my country and life was all about money and winning. But to me it wasn't just about these things, it was also about creating something that you could be proud of, something you could stamp your name and reputation on.

'A lot of people that I have met through my life thought being an entrepreneur was all about greed and money. They couldn't be more wrong. Yes, the money is a scorecard of success, but knowing that you have made a difference is the most fulfilling thing. The real reward is creating a difference to your team's life, your clients' businesses, your own integrity and growth as an individual.

'When I set out it was about survival and controlling my own destiny, it was about dreaming big dreams . . . 15 years later I have achieved most of those dreams, living on the beach, owning my own helicopter, driving Porsches and Ferraris, not having to work every day. I have been very lucky but I've put in lot of hard work. I have a lot of people to thank for all of their help and belief in me because I couldn't have done any of this without them.

'Would I have changed becoming an entrepreneur? No way–it's been worth every late night, sleepless night and early morning–the satisfaction of creating a successful company and team is something that no one can ever take away.

'Good luck–and remember it's not just about the end goal–it's about the journey. Have FUN and SMILE!'

Adam Miller, *Group Chief Executive, ELEVATE*

Vision, purpose and personal mission statement

Now we need to define where you want to be. To help you answer this, think about what your passion is in life. What were you put on this earth to do? It doesn't mean what you are better at than anyone else, or what can you make lots of money from. It is about what makes you tick. You don't have to have an answer right away, but your ultimate success in life will be determined by your ability to clearly define this. Once we know what it is, we can make a plan to deliver it, maybe through the path of entrepreneurship and maybe not – whichever you choose is the right choice for you, for now!

Vision

'We can change our lives. We can do, have, and be exactly what we wish. The path to success is to take massive, determined action.

One reason so few of us achieve what we truly want is that we never direct our focus; we never concentrate our power. Most people dabble their way through life, never deciding to master anything in particular.'

Tony Robbins

I discovered long ago what I was put on this earth to do but it took me quite a while to see the light. Probably because I didn't have the benefit of a process to help me identify what was right for me. I drifted around until I ended up realizing that I was indeed a pure bred entrepreneur. Nothing else in life was going to make me as happy. This wasn't a straightforward choice. It wasn't just about being an entrepreneur; it was contributing back into the system, helping other would-be entrepreneurs, that was my motivation and passion. That's where I get the real buzz.

It was not until recently that I discovered that knowing what you want is one thing, but actually articulating that vision and putting a plan together to get there was quite another. The universe will conspire to help you reach your ultimate goal, but you need to help it on its way by documenting and acting upon a detailed plan.

For me my ultimate goal is attaining 'freedom' – this simple word was my life vision! From cars, to money, to business, to my partner; everything was geared towards the same thing – I had never really worked out this fact before, but after I did my life accelerated 1000% faster towards what makes me happy!

The power of 'purpose'

Without a purpose in life, it's easy to get sidetracked on your life's journey. It's easy to wander and drift, accomplishing little. With a purpose, however, everything in life seems to fall into place. To be 'on purpose' means you're doing what you love to do, doing what you're good at and accomplishing what's important to you.

I am testament to the fact that If you can achieve clarity around your purpose then the people, resources, and opportunities you need naturally gravitate toward you. As we have said before, you need to help it along the way with a clearly defined path of practical and achievable goals; but don't underestimate the power of focusing on your life purpose.

In his book *The Success Principles*, Jack Canfield tells us that in order to create a balanced and successful life, your vision needs to include the following seven areas:

1. work and career;
2. finances;
3. recreation and free time;
4. health and fitness;
5. relationships;
6. personal goals; and
7. contribution to the larger community.

Think about each of these areas before moving on.

Personal Mission Statement – the future is . . . whatever colour I decide

> *'If you don't set your goals based upon your mission statement, you may be climbing the ladder of success only to realize, when you get to the top, you're on the WRONG BUILDING.'*
> **Stephen Covey:** *7 Habits of Highly Effective People*

You may have heard about mission statements before. Most companies will have one, articulating their ultimate objective and ethos. This then becomes the touchstone for everything they do and every path they take. It should require no explanation and should motivate everyone in the same direction. When Stephen Covey talks about *mission statement* in this quote he is referring to the articulation of your life purpose. We have talked about how important it is to have a clear vision of where you want to be, and a personal mission statement is putting this into words. When you have done this you will be able to create a set of clear goals in line with it.

Much like a company mission statement it should require no further explanation, but should motivate you every time you look at it . . . and you should look at it regularly. Frame it and put it up on your wall if necessary.

What should you include when writing a great personal mission statement?

1. Draft a hand-written or typed-out paragraph
2. Describe your best characteristics and how you express them.
3. Have specific, measurable outcomes.
4. Set a deadline – for example, December 31st.

How *not* to write your mission statement:

> 'I aspire to start my own business. I want to help others and be a better businesswoman. I will deliver the best food with the highest service levels.' Jane

This example is too general – it doesn't explain the person's unique qualities, has no goal or deadline and could apply to just about anyone.

Q: How do I go about creating my Personal Mission Statement?

A: A mission statement is defined as having goals and a deadline. This is opposed to the notion that a mission statement is just a bunch of flowery, general phrases like, 'I will be the best business person I can be.'

A much more powerful mission statement would state:

> 'I will start my business within 3 months and plan to grow it to £500,000 in revenues within a year. Using this success my staff and I will spread the

word to local schools and businesses about eco-friendly food production in order that we reach at least 100 people within the same time frame. My purpose will be to massively add value to our local community in measurable ways that have a real impact on people's health now and in the future'

Q: What are some simple steps to goal setting after creating a mission statement?

A: You must base your goals upon your mission statement. If you've created your mission statement according to the process above, you'll now have 'big' goals to achieve by one year from today. From there, you'll need to break them down into quarterly, monthly and even weekly goals.

Your Personal Mission Statement:

Jane's:
Vision

I see my life free from the corporate shackles and am working for myself. I am bringing happiness to customers and family alike with my cooking and recipes. I am also educating people in the importance of healthy organic food that hasn't had to travel thousands of miles to get to their plate. I am changing the eating habits of a generation of kids.

My Personal Mission Statement

I will start my business within 3 months and plan to grow it to £500,000 in revenues within a year. Using this success my staff and I will spread the word to local schools and businesses about eco-friendly food production in order that we reach at least 100 people within the same time frame. My purpose will be to massively add value to our local community in measurable ways that have a real impact on people's health now and in the future.

Don't be too worried about this being perfect or even finished. The key here is to just think about it and have some ideas about your bigger goals in life. Use this to compare with your business idea and see if there is a fit.

INSIDER TIP

Creating a personal vision and mission is a big topic and I can't cover it in enough detail in this book but please take the time to explore it in your own time.

An excellent work book to help with this process is "The Personal Vision Workbook" by Tobin Burgess et al.

Identifying personal criteria that will fit your new business

Among the many things to think about when you're trying to decide what kind of business you're going to start, you need to consider how different businesses will fit your *lifestyle* and your interests and meet other personal criteria. As you now have a clear view on what you want out of life and your resources, you should be able to easily decide on the correct business for you.

You will now know that being your own boss is very demanding, but the flip side is that you can make your own decisions and control your own destiny. This great flexibility is one of the major reasons people become entrepreneurs, and if you're the parent of small children; you probably want a business that allows you to have this flexibility. School plays, open days and other events that will pop up in the middle of the day – those kinds of things just shouldn't be missed.

Consider some other examples:

- If being close to your family is a top priority, consider a business that can be operated from your home.
- If you're a high-powered, ambitious sort, you should look for a business with lots of growth potential, where you can create something that is as big as your dreams.
- If you've retired from a job and want to start a business to keep you busy while earning a little extra money, you might want to consider something that requires only part-time hours.
- If you love warm weather or being outside, then look for a business that can give you what you need or consider moving somewhere that offers the right climate.

Also, take into account your personal and family situations, your financial needs, your health, your personality, your work habits, and other factors that may be particularly relevant to you.

Think about your work habits and body clock. Are you a person who loves to hang around the office until 10 or 11 at night or do you get your best work done before 6 a.m.? Some businesses lend themselves better to particular hours than others, and it's worth thinking about how your business hours and your personal hours will eventually mesh. You should also try and match your passions and interests with some or the entire role you will take in your new business.

In short, brainstorm all these issues and not just the core business idea in order to give yourself the best long term chance of success. Of course, I'm not suggesting you set out to create a business just to satisfy your personal whims either, but I do believe it's important to have a business that deals with things you like. Believing in what you're doing makes you a better businessperson. And it's a lot more fun doing something that you love than something that's just another product.

It's not all about the 'money' or being a 'millionaire'

'If you are starting a business to get rich then don't. There are easier ways to get rich: become an investment banker, a hedge fund manager or a senior executive. You must want independence, control over your life or some overriding ambition to change the world. Nothing less will sustain you over the long haul.'

Doug Richard, *Dragons' Den*

What an interesting idea – 'to be rich' – what does that mean? How do you define rich? What do you do to get riches? What is the result of being rich? These are questions we should all ask ourselves if we are to set out on the entrepreneurial path.

The funny thing about the answers to these questions for me is that they are very different, depending upon who you ask.

If you ask my rich friends (those that have material wealth), many will say that they strived for riches to get freedom. However, the more money they get the less free they feel . . . an interesting paradox. If you ask the many wannabes or those trying to get rich, they say it's all about the money. Those with money often cite health and youth as 'riches' while the young covet the money their older and wealthier idols have sitting in their bank accounts.

Who is right and what are 'riches'?

To me, material wealth is simply a trade-off. As you get wealthier the cost of this financial gain is usually a significant loss of time, energy and health.

When you are in your teens (when I started) and then your 20s and maybe even early 30s you see a very long road ahead, and your body seems to have an unlimited shelf life – even when you abuse it regularly – but as you toil away towards your material goals you start to wake up to the costs.

Very few in this world can have lots of free time, incredible health, a stress-free existence and lots of money. Money usually extracts its toll on these things, and yet many of us want the former and think the latter will deliver it to them!

For me, real riches are about doing what you love and getting paid for it – how much is immaterial. Many of my friends are very wealthy indeed, but some have very little money in comparison. I always find those with the least financial wealth seem happiest and often have a really 'rich' life – full of joy, happiness and love. The same is not true for many of my wealthy friends!

So maybe the question should be – what kind of riches do you want?!

In my life I often find myself answering the question: when you retire and get really rich what will you do? My answer is quite funny if you think about it. I say, 'I will sit on my boat in my shorts and fish'. The funny thing is that when I travel around the world I see the poorest people I come across all doing just this . . .! Here I am chasing around, working all hours, sacrificing so many things to get the same thing that some of the poorest people I have ever met already have. The fact is, they are the richest in so many ways even if they don't know it.

So if you are clever you will follow your passion and not the money – this will deliver all the 'riches' you will ever need.

Make an 'I want' list

So, what kind of riches do you want?

Once you have decided why you are here, you have to decide what you *want* to do, be, and have. What do you *want* to accomplish? What do you *want* to experience? In the journey from where you are now to where you *want* to be, you have to decide what exactly what that destination is. In other words, what does success look like to you?

As we have outlined already, one of the main reasons why most people don't get what they want is that they haven't actually *decided* what they want. They haven't defined their desires in clear and compelling detail.

When I was sixteen and starting on my entrepreneurial journey I found real inspiration in the following quote and have lived by it ever since (and it's proved true for me):

'YOU GOTTA BELIEVE'

'You can be anything you want to be, if only you believe with sufficient conviction and act in accordance with your faith; for <u>whatever the mind can conceive and believe, the mind can achieve</u>.'

Napoleon Hill, *best-selling author of*
Think and Grow Rich

One of the easiest ways to begin clarifying what you truly want is to make a list of 30 things you want to do, 30 things you want to have, and 30 things you want to be before you die. This is a great way to get the ball rolling.

Another powerful technique to unearth your wants is to ask a friend to help you make an 'I want' list. Have your friend continually ask, 'What do you want? What do you want?' for 10 to 15 minutes, and jot down your answers. You'll find the first 'wants' aren't all that profound. In fact, most people usually hear themselves saying, 'I want a Mercedes. I want a big house by the ocean' . . . and so on. However, by the end of the 15-minute exercise, the real you begins to speak: 'I want people to love me. I want to express myself. I want to make a difference. I want to feel powerful'. You will discover that these ultimate 'wants' are true expressions of your core values.

INSIDER TIP

There is nothing wrong with wanting material things like a nice car and home, but try and make sure you balance that with things that are deeper and really important.

The deeper things are harder to define and find but they are equally as important.

Also, make sure that whenever you list a "want" whatever it may be that its very clear in your mind and try and visualise it regularly, daily if you can, as if you have already achieved it. This will bring the power of your subconscious mind to help you, a powerful ally.

The 'I want' list

Jane's:

- I want to create a highly profitable and successful home and small business catering company.
- I want a chain of companies with a really strong brand.
- I want a great house in the countryside where I grew up.
- I want recognition from friends and family.
- I want my friends and family to benefit from my business.
- I want to create a family business that my siblings and later my children can go into.
- I want to look after my family.
- I want to spend time with my family . . . CHA . . . it works—I am not as shallow as I thought!?.

> - *I want a life filled with excitement and contribution.*
> - *I ultimately want to find love, happiness and fulfilment.*

Now make this list into a set of goals by making them into a list with specific outcomes, timescales and a purpose behind them.

Your specific goals and actions:

Jane's:

- *I want to create a catering company with £250K profits in three years' time. Achieving this will not only give me the freedom and excitement but will be a great reward for my hard work. It will also enable me to help out family and friends while putting money aside for my retirement.*
- *I want to hire up to 30 people in three years' time, whose skills and knowledge will complement my own and who believe as passionately as I do about the importance of organic healthy eating, especially for children.*
- *I want each of my family to have a role in the company over the next five years either as a member of staff or as an adviser in some capacity to try and create that feeling of a family business.*

Now what about the *type* of life you want to lead?

Lifestyle considerations

Jane's:

I am an early bird and love to get up at the crack of dawn and start cooking, and at the end of the day I like to have free time to read and relax rather at home. I am planning on having a family and so having a flexible work routine in the future would also be great. I also need to think carefully about financial plans and work hours to fit in with the costs of the business and an expanding home.

Congratulations! You should now have a plan, goals, a clear understanding of who you are and your resources. Your passions and plans should be matched to your business dreams and you should be feeling excited about your future.

The next step is to take the 'big decision', but before you do let's make sure you don't caught out by any hidden fears that may be in the back of your mind.

Mentor Session 6

Is it Really for Me?

- Getting over the fear of starting out
- Anyone can become an entrepreneur at any life stage
- The young or 'student' entrepreneur
- Making the transition from the corporate world
- Geriatrapreneur
- Top ten excuses for not becoming an entrepreneur
- Lessons

'Far better is it to dare mighty things, to win glorious triumphs even though checkered by failure than to take rank with those poor spirits who neither enjoy much nor suffer much because they live in the grey twilight that knows neither victory nor defeat'.

Theodore Roosevelt

We are getting down to the final decision now. You know what you love to do in life, your skills, resources, vision, life mission and goals. Now it's time to take the plunge, you may feel a little nervous. This feeling of fear is only natural if you are about to make a decision where you don't really know what will happen – a big decision with its attendant risks. But don't worry – I am here to keep working with you through this; it's not half as difficult when you are as prepared as you are!

Getting over the fear of starting out

Wikipedia defines it as: 'Fear is an emotional response to impending danger that is tied to anxiety.'

The way to deal with uncertainty, fear and doubt is to analyse it. Part of the problem with a fear or doubt is often that it's actually a mixture of several issues or concerns; these are probably not clearly defined or weighted as to their severity – adding to the confusion.

So let's address this by looking at the most common reasons people cite for not taking the plunge and see how you relate to them – allowing you to rationalize your fear and make a sensible decision. Let's consider why you might decide not to become an entrepreneur and judge if it really should stop you. One of the top issues people often have is their age and life stage; they think they are too young, too old or stuck in a family situation preventing them from starting a business. Let's look at that first.

Anyone can become an entrepreneur at any life stage

A person may choose to become an entrepreneur at any stage of life. It is possible to start an entrepreneurial venture from virtually any point. Entrepreneurs start new ventures while at school, college or university, after completing their education, during times of unemployment, from the home, or from existing businesses.

Think of these possibilities as starting points:

- Part-time at school;
- Part-time at university, targeting the off-campus or on-campus markets;
- After graduating, with a developed business plan;
- After resigning from a job, or after being laid off;
- After retirement;
- After leaving a job, but with advanced preparation for a business venture completed while still employed, either as a natural outgrowth from job-related duties and contracts or completely unrelated to previous job duties; or
- After moonlighting with a part-time business on weekends or evenings.

The young or 'student' entrepreneur

'For me, being young is definitely an advantage! Being young and successful has given me great confidence to believe in what can be achieved and with our business, it is really important to understand the needs of the users who range from 18 to 80, so I think that being young means that you remain more versatile to change, which is happening

> *all the time in social networking and the entrepreneurial*
> *world. As long as you're innovative, ambitious and believe*
> *in what you are doing – anything is possible!'*
>
> **Peter Ward,** *CEO Wayn*

Many people think they are too young, but the key point related to being too young or not is probably more related to 'maturity'. Are you eighteen but you think and act like an adult, or are you still going from one thing to another, lacking the ability to take responsibility for your life? When I was eighteen I was really desperate to start a business. I read many books about it and took the whole thing very seriously – that made me a mature young person, and as a result I had credibility.

According to a 1997 Gallup study, 7 out of 10 high school students say they want to start their own business. Starting and running your own business while still in school is a great opportunity to grow, learn, network, and accumulate wealth. However, only a tiny proportion of students actually start a business. Because of a lack of direct experience with entrepreneurship, students develop unfounded beliefs about it that can stop them from starting a company.

Advantages of being a young entrepreneur

- Invulnerability   Although it may be argued whether this is an advantage or not, youth means minimal past exposure to failure. Invulnerability is a natural feeling when you're young. Lack of exposure to failure makes younger people feel invincible and willing to take risks until something happens to teach them otherwise.

- Limited responsibility

While you are young your level and degree of responsibility is still minimal. In most cases, students aren't married, don't have children, and don't own a home. Financial loss should not be enough of a reason to fear starting your own business, and one can live on very little or take help from family.

- You gain experience and increase your value

Owning and running your own business is an incredible way to gain experience and credentials regardless of whether you decide to stay in business or take a job once you graduate. Whether you like it or not, you will have to learn about business and what makes the world go around. An employer will also value the fact that you had the enthusiasm and confidence to do your own thing. Put simply, starting a business as a student increases your 'value' in the marketplace, sets you apart and gives you more options. The worst thing that could happen if your business fails is that you get a job, have an incredible credential on your CV, and have experience that will increase your chances of success in the future.

• You develop networking skills	You've likely heard that your network increases your net worth. Consider the fact that by running a business and constantly being in a business community, you will develop excellent contacts. If you choose to get a job after you graduate, you will have a great set of friends and colleagues who will be more likely to hire you.
• You will learn more about yourself and what they don't teach at school	Entrepreneurship is the combination of all the disciplines of business. It includes knowledge of sales, marketing, accounting, management and operations. Already having knowledge of these topics before you take classes on them allows you to see more clearly how everything fits together. Also, you will be able to learn early-on what subjects you like so you can make better decisions on your career or next step in education.

Disadvantages of being a young entrepreneur

Young entrepreneurs also face some disadvantageous issues when starting a new business, such as lack of credibility, lack of experience, leadership challenges and motivation.

• Lack of credibility	It's one thing for your friends to attest to your credibility, but it's another to convince a potential vendor, customer, or banker that you're a good risk.

There are a many ways to gain credibility. The main one is having an air of self-confidence (but not arrogance), showing others that you are determined to succeed. It's sometimes hard to resist believing someone who is so driven and ambitious.

Maturity is the key when you are young and also having a good network that can attest to your reliability will help. Of course, having a 'grey hair' on the team can also mitigate most of these issues.

- Not enough experience

When you're young, some people will assume that you can't be old enough to know what you're doing. They may be right! But you show your maturity by being honest about your weak points and how you have set about fixing them – for example, if you are not so good at accounting then hire a part-time bookkeeper. You will probably be really good at some things and they are also things to emphasize.

- Lack of leadership skills

If you are going to start your own company, you are going to have to rely largely on your skills as a leader. Even if you won't be starting off with a staff, you are going to have to be very comfortable with being in charge. Once again, you can illustrate your leadership through previous project experience, say at school. Or you may just have to learn on the job and discover your own talents in this area.

• Motivation

As motivated as you might be to make your business a success, you will not always have that surge of enthusiasm when you wake up in the morning. When your buddies are out having fun and you have a ton of work still to do, it can be tough to knuckle down and get on with it when you are young. Since you don't have a boss, you won't have someone pushing you to get moving, and you will need to learn to be disciplined or you will soon not have a business.

Most of the biggest technology success stories have been made by founders who were in their 20s and the peak age was 26. Bill Gates was 20 when he started Microsoft. Steve Jobs was 21 when he created Apple with Steve Wozniak (25). The Google guys were both 25 when they launched their business.

INSIDER TIP

I started at 18, I loved it and found it fun and rewarding to start my business – against the advice of my career advisor at college.

Don't let anyone stop you starting out because of your age, in today's day and age it's even easier than over 20 years ago when I did it.

Making the transition from the corporate world

The majority of today's entrepreneurs will probably have had some work experience and be making the leap from job to self-employment.

Even though you have probably been programmed throughout your life by parents, friends, and most of the people around you to get a job and become one of the company's greatest assets, you can change whenever you want – it's your life!

Firstly let's take a look at the differences between an employee and entrepreneur. The table shows the difference in roles and mindset between an entrepreneur and an employee.

Consideration	Entrepreneurs	Employees
Job security	Value freedom over job security. Own the company. Can only be fired by Board of Directors. Have a higher tolerance for risk.	Value job security over freedom. Could be fired at any time. Averse to risk.
The corporate ladder	No corporate ladder and hopefully very little politics.	Have to climb the ladder and lots of politics.
Salary	Can go months or years without payment. Once the business is successful pay can be more generous but	Receive consistent pay cheque and often annual raises. Build active income, taxed the highest. Constant

	most make their money when they get an exit or sale. Build passive *(a business that makes money for you without your direct involvement)* and portfolio income *(combination of a number of different business interests)*, taxed lowest. Potential for very large payoff	wages but smaller payoff if it all goes well.
Lifestyle	Often have to dedicate yourself fully during start-up stages. Hard to raise a family and start a high-potential venture.	Have time to do other things besides work– such as raise a family or take up hobbies.
Hours	Long hours, especially during start-up. Can have a very flexible work life and hours.	Regular, consistent hours, little flexibility.
Job benefits	Provide your own, can be without any benefits until successful.	Medical, dental, insurances, holiday pay, expenses etc.
Responsibility	Total responsibility (staff, investors, family) that can be daunting.	Whatever goes with your job, but if things go wrong you have the company safety net.
Assets growth/ pension	Work on building assets so they'll never need a pension.	Work on building pension.
Work colleagues	Decides who to hire and who they work with.	Have little say over who they work with.
Personal growth	Are able to use all of their skill sets.	Use only a small portion of their abilities.
Flexibility	Adapt quickly to change.	Often resist change.

Variety	Rarely do the same thing two days in a row.	Often have repetitive jobs.
Control/destiny	Have freedom to control direction of their company.	Have little say over the direction of their company.
Financial security	Financial security once venture succeeds.	Will have to follow strict saving and investment plan to reach financial security by retirement.
Job outcome	Build their own assets.	Work to build someone else's assets.
Commitment	Total, or the business will fail.	Can get away with low commitment.
Cultures	Low politics (hopefully) with a faster pace and more nimble ability to adapt.	High in politics, slower and more procedurally driven.

Keep in mind, even if the job market is great – if you don't want to be in it, you probably won't be in it for long, as your subconscious mind could well sabotage your efforts to be a good employee! Also, remember that as valuable a commodity as you may be today, there are many people right behind you, just as anxious to benefit from a good education, strike out on their own, and take over your job perhaps for less money and with better skills to offer. <u>No one can fire you from a business you control and own</u>.

If you choose to make the change and jump off the corporate hamster wheel it will be a big shock, especially if you were in management at a typical big corporation.

On the negative side, I am sorry to tell you that entrepreneurship may mean:

- No regular money and maybe some big debts;
- Loss of social status (or possibly more depending on your friends);
- Lots of stress and pressure;
- Pressure on your relationships;
- Lack of sleep and very long tiring hours;
- No more IT dept, admin staff to run around after you and very little 'people power' to propel you;
- Loss of the expensive company car, the house, the long holidays and the security . . .

Of course, on the plus side:

- Freedom;
- Independence;
- Self reliance; and
- Maybe, just maybe, a big pay day.

Before you take the plunge and submit your resignation from your corporate job however, consider the following final pieces of advice:

- Know what you're getting into – being ready for things to look, feel, and sound completely foreign will increase your odds of navigating the massive changes.
- No more structure – small companies are much more flexible and fast moving.
- Check your motivation – hating your job is not by itself a good reason to start a business.
- Start a business on the side – make sure you are enjoying it before leaving behind your regular pay cheque.
- Get advice about what it's really like – talk to people in the same industry.
- Get a job at a start-up before you start a start-up.
- Be financially prepared – have at least a year's costs in the bank.

- Don't be afraid to fail.
- Brace yourself – be prepared for the ups and downs and all the issues that go with momentous change.
- Once you're in, you can't get out – an entrepreneur's business becomes a core part of their life and they often constantly think about it – hence the many references to it being 'like a mistress'!

INSIDER TIP

Starting a business with experience of a market or various job roles is an obvious advantage and you must make sure you take full advantage.

Make sure you leverage your colleagues, network and history before you leave your job to speed you on your way in the early days.

You may even have a supportive boss who will help. So you never know, make sure you ask at the right time!

You can be an 'geriatrepreneur' when you are over 55 too

Jonathan Mudd, founder of The Real Crisps Company, is a great example of a success story for someone later in life. He started his business in his early fifties because he felt he needed to go for it with few second chances at his age.

'It was a bit scary and several people told me it was a brave thing to do at my time of life. But I thought it was a good plan. I also thought that if I left Bensons, there wouldn't be a queue of people waiting to offer me a job, so I had better do something for myself.'

It used to be that when someone turned 55, he or she was considered on a downhill slide towards retirement and unemployment. Now people in their 50s realize they've got a lot left to offer, and much experience, and they're spending their time, not thinking about retirement, but figuring out what they want to do with the second half of their adult life.

Many in this age bracket are 'empty nesters' who have the time and energy to devote to a new calling. Many have also realized that after years in the corporate world, they want more flexibility and the opportunity to be rewarded in a more direct manner for their work efforts.

Whether your goal is to create wealth, to give back and help others or to stay busy and creative, more and more people over 55 are thinking of pursuing the entrepreneurial path.

But being older does have a different set of issues to consider:

- Being comfortable doing all levels of tasks
- After spending years in the corporate world, you may be used to delegating many tasks. You need to carefully consider whether you'll be OK sweeping the floor as well as making the decisions.
- Putting your personal assets at risk
- Most people have accumulated substantial assets by the time they're in their mid-50s and may be significantly less willing to risk those assets. Carefully consider what resources you're willing to use in financing your business (especially retirement account assets) before setting out.
- Changing your lifestyle
- Many baby boomers reaching 55 have decided they want a more flexible lifestyle that allows for additional time off, travel opportunities or other priorities. When you are investigating potential businesses, make sure to consider your lifestyle concerns.

- Preparing exit plans
- Time can be an important factor as you get older; and you need to decide how much longer you want to work and what you're going to do with the business when you reach the point where you don't want to run it any more. Whether you want to sell, or turn a business over to your heirs, you should definitely begin the process with this in mind.

You can experience tremendous joy and fulfilment during the process of 'reinventing' yourself later in life. You get a wonderful second chance to build a life that has more meaning for you, and that can also be financially rewarding. Like any other age group, all you need to do is take the time to really think through what you want out of business ownership and then investigate all opportunities carefully to make sure you select one that provides what's important to you.

Are you still finding reasons why being an entrepreneur is not for you? Excluding age and life stage, let's deal with those nagging doubts and try and help you get over any issues you may have in your way. Let's take a look at the top excuses people use for not taking the leap, and see if we can dispel any unfounded fears you may still have about becoming an entrepreneur.

Top ten excuses for not becoming an entrepreneur

1 'I am afraid of being an entrepreneur as it's risky and I could fail'

According to most statistics, the majority of businesses fail financially after the first few years. The bottom line is that it's OK to fail so long as you learn and improve each time.

Napoleon Hill said that his research of the great entrepreneurs of his time showed 'every failure has within it the seeds for equal or greater success. It is your decision whether you plant these seeds'.

I have failed more times that I can remember, but each time I have used these failures as opportunities, learning more from when I failed then when I succeeded. Sometimes it's really hard to get back on the saddle, if you have had a major disappointment or your business has collapsed. Indeed, some people I know just couldn't recover and went back to an employed job – but we who are in this life for the long term brush ourselves off, recover quickly and move on.

The other key thing to know is that with a little confidence you will actually embrace mini-failures or market tests as a way to reduce risk.

"Fail fast and fail often" is another saying. In other words, just get started and try something, but if it looks as though you chose the wrong idea, get out before you waste too much time or money on it. Or perhaps change the idea based on your learning.

If you decide you want to go back into the corporate world you will find future employers recognize the strength in failure. Failure shows courage – as long as your failure was market-led rather than incompetence!

Nor will investors hold it against you, as long as you didn't fail by being greedy, lazy or dishonest – it's part of the game for them and they expect a large portion of their investments to fail.

The bottom line is that you will not be considered a real failure if you did your best, gave it your all, and acted with honesty and integrity.

When I interview people enamoured by their degrees, I doubt if they've got the chutzpah for the start-up world.

You don't need an MBA

The process of starting a business is sloppy, rough, and messy, and whether someone has an M.B.A. is the last thing on my mind. An M.B.A. is all about learning the structured and bureaucratic rules of business. Traditional business schools teach students to value position and lines of authority. Ironically, authority and bureaucracy are meaningless in the start-up world, where <u>creativity, struggle, and sacrifice reign supreme</u>.

An M.B.A. won't keep you from succeeding as an entrepreneur, of course. The key is to understand the difference between the skills you studied in school and those you'll need to start a business. Not surprisingly, many of the world's greatest entrepreneurs don't have college degrees, much less M.B.A.s.

Stuart Skorman, *serial entrepreneur, founder of empire video and reel.com*

2 'I don't have a degree – I'm not clever enough to be an entrepreneur'

Excellent – nor do I. I have never had any kind of third level education. Never stopped me.

Don't get me wrong – you do need to be a smart and have a certain aptitude for learning. Like many successful entrepreneurs I just didn't want to go to university. I wanted to work for myself! You don't necessarily need that specialist with a degree or M.B.A. For my own part I do read a great deal, especially when I want to learn something new or understand something – I am not afraid to learn and I am very curious.

Evidence suggests that most self-made millionaires have average intelligence. Nonetheless, these people reached their full potential and achieved their financial and personal goals in business because they were willing to learn. To succeed, you must be willing to ask questions, remain curious and open to new knowledge. This is even more crucial given the rapid changes in technologies and ways of doing business. Become a student of business best practices. You will want to learn and emulate other businesses and strategies that have been successful.

There are many examples throughout history of super-successful people with little or no education. Charles Merrill (Merrill Lynch), started college, but he was forced to drop out because of a lack of funds. Still, he made his way to Wall Street and was rich by his 31st birthday. Henry Ford not only didn't have much formal education himself, but he had a general distrust of college graduates, even those that worked for him. Walt Disney's education was leaving home at age sixteen to join the Red Cross Ambulance Corps during the First World War. Similiarly with McDonald's hamburger guru Ray Kroc; in fact, Kroc was only fifteen and lied about his age.

<u>It's not about being conventionally clever, it's about providing customers with something they need and providing a better service than anyone else</u>. As we have already learnt, as an entrepreneur your skill set will actually have to be broader than working for a corporate.

It's also more about hard work, not giving up, being dedicated, learning from your mistakes. If you need specialized knowledge, then you can get it or recruit a team member to do it for you.

Clever entrepreneurs 'hire' clever people.

3 'I don't have any money s⟨ become an entrepreneur'

I started my first business, excluding aⁿ school, with £500 loan from my father when I waₛ my second business with the sale proceeds of my car, others with tiny bank loans or my credit card.

Depending on your ambitions and the type of business you want to start, you don't need lots of capital. If you've got somewhere to sleep and enough money to travel and to eat you have enough money to start your own business. Clearly, if you have a family then you will need more of a financial cushion.

To compensate for a low budget, you have to be creative, resourceful, and make realistic plans. All of which will stand you in good stead for your life as an entrepreneur. You will be amazed what you can achieve with very little, an enterprising spirit and the help of others.

Of course, if you plan to launch a capital-intensive business it will take a little longer, as you will need the immediate support of others such as banks or investors.

Money chases great ideas and great spirit.

4 'I want to be a millionaire, so I will become an entrepreneur'

It's fine to dream about a better life and want to improve your personal financial circumstances, but this should not be the focus of your start-up efforts or your path as an entrepreneur. Rarely does anyone succeed by being self-serving or chasing money. In order to succeed you need to add value to others, and money is a by-product of being great at doing that.

u should have a greater purpose or goal, and execute
nat to the best of your ability – focus your passions and
enthusiasm on your business, or choose a business that
enables you to do that more easily by aligning the business
with your own life vision.

Those who are super-successful at anything in life seem
to do it effortlessly, and that's often because they are
acting 'on-purpose' and totally love what they do – this
then leads to excellence above others and excellence in
anything leads to financial reward. This is the only way
round you should think about becoming a millionaire as
an entrepreneur.

5 'I don't have a hot idea'

Having an idea is great, and in reality you don't need a 'hot'
one – just a focus on something you want to do that you are
passionate and excited about.

Almost invariably the initial idea an entrepreneur has is
not the one that makes the money. The trick is to take
any reasonably good idea in a growth market in which
you have skills, experience and contacts and just get
going.

Once you have started down the road you should let the
market dictate your direction, and when you come to that
fork in the road where it's a choice between your original
idea and what your customers actually want, then you will
have to make a judgment call about the 'hottest idea'.

In the final analysis it will all be about the execution and
the team, rather than the idea.

Almost all investors back great people before great ideas.

6 'My parents want me to become an astronaut (or whatever) . . .

A significant number of would-be entrepreneurs are probably dissuaded from doing it by their parents who have always had a vision of the life they want for their offspring.

However, the problem with parents could be that they are not in 'tune' with you and what you want, or they are still more interested in their own fears and historical biases than what's true in the world today.

My parents always wanted me to be a bio-technician or something similar, until it was obvious I was going to do my own thing whatever happened. They didn't try and hold me back but they didn't really have the understanding to guide me either.

You need to consider your own goals, objectives and needs rather than those of your family before making a decision. Then you should try and communicate these with your nearest and dearest and have them come on your side and support you in your quest. If they are set in their ways and try and dissuade you, then try and form an independent view about what's best for you personally.

7 'Why don't I just get (stay in) a job like everyone else? Why become an entrepreneur?

We have examined the benefits of being an entrepreneur, and by now it should be clear if that type of life is a fit for you personally. Of course, you can get on or off the job ladder as you wish. You could go from school straight to a job or a start-up – it's up to you. If you do choose to do your own thing it will be probably be because you have a dream you want to fulfil, but if it doesn't work out you can always go on to get a job later, like me!

Many successful entrepreneurs I know have spent some of their early years 'learning the ropes' as company employees before branching out on their own. It's just not cut and dried, and luckily you can decide to do it now, or get a job and do it later. Or perhaps you have decided that from your reading of this book, a 'career' is going to be the best thing for you.

8 'I have a family to feed, so I can't become an entrepreneur'

There is no doubt that having family responsibilities is a real challenge. Those monthly expenses won't just go away, and not everyone will be happy when the annual holiday gets the chop due to financial or time pressure.

The things to consider in this position are, how to reduce the risks and how to avoid the pain that goes with failing. I always encourage people in this position to ensure the strong support of their family, have some money to fall back upon when the going gets tough, and have a clear outcome in mind. Don't just jump into it like you are someone much younger – it's better to plan, test and then take a calculated risk.

Start small, start on weekends, evenings, prove it works without spending a lot of money and be cautious. Get your family to support you, get them involved, and make it fun. You can have a lot of fun achieving something that you dream of, and sharing those dreams is even better with someone you love.

If you and your partner share the excitement of your vision, then you can work together on a plan to share responsibilities of bringing in household cash before your business provides you with enough household income.

9 'I am not experienced in business'

You don't need to know anything about 'business' to start a start-up. However, if you do have these skills then all the better.

The key here is self-awareness. If you know what you are good at, then focus on that and get a partner or a team together with the skills that are missing. It will definitely help you avoid some big holes if you can get someone with related experience mentoring you, or being directly involved from an early stage; but it's not essential, just more efficient and with lower risk.

When you first start out you should be more concerned with getting the idea to a stage where you can get it funded or get some customers. Once you get some revenues in you can iron out the wrinkles of the business.

I have always found that if you are prepared to listen, learn and read you will be able to pick up all the skills you need as you go along!

10 'I don't have a partner or team to support me'

Not having a co-founder or a team can be a problem. A start-up is a lot for one person to handle for very long. All investors, without exception, are more likely to fund you with a team (or at least a co-founder) than without. Of course, it depends on the scale of the operation. Many micro-businesses can be set up by one person and expanded later on.

If your venture is more ambitious, try and get a team together as soon as you can. It can be hard to get a team together quickly from scratch, so this is an area where forward planning and working for someone else before you launch can help. If you have work colleagues, friends and others in your network you can start to sound them out before you get going building a skeleton team, and have them ready to jump on board when the time is right.

Finding the courage to go for it

'The important thing is not being afraid to take a chance. Remember, the greatest failure is to not try. Once you find something you love to do, be the best at doing it.'
Debbi Fields, *founder of Mrs Fields' Cookies*

As you should see, the challenges of becoming an entrepreneur are not that great or risky with a bit of planning and thinking. Even if you fail once or twice, it's all part of the ride. Adopt that attitude and it will seem so much less scary.

An entrepreneurial spirit would not be daunted by all the challenges presented in our learning so far, so I'm sure yours has not been. It's important to understand what being an entrepreneur entails, but it's also important to try and see the positive in those things. Hard work, long hours, responsibility, and financial considerations should be looked upon as challenges that you'll have great fun tackling and overcoming.

Forget the notion that you need some unique education, power, connections, or money to be an entrepreneur. If you really want own your own business, you have everything it takes.

Stop dreaming about it and do it today!
Dreams only come true with action. The time will never be perfect. Your finances will never be what you want them to be. Your children will never be old enough. Whatever reasons you have been using not to get started or for not doing as well in business as you could, must be confronted honestly.

Fear is normal but, if you ever plan to own your own successful business, the time has never been better. There are more support systems and more information for small businesses – and more acceptance of them than ever before.

Success does not happen overnight, but it does happen. You are in control of whether it happens for you.

Lessons

Take the 'rocking chair' test before you give up on your dream

Before you either give up on your dream or if you are starting along its path, this is a fantastic way to consider your future and to give you a perspective.

Consider yourself at a ripe old age, sitting with your grandchildren at your knee. What will you tell them about your life? Did you take the rocky path and come out successful and fulfilled? Did you let others determine your destiny? Did you overcome immense odds and achieve your dreams, or were you happy just doing your job? Test your dreams; do you want to be someone special who has exciting stories to relate about your long life, or is it better to have a pension plan and nice home?

What a great way to run a business – this is a message Howies T-shirt company sends with a new garment:

100% Organic Cotton

This product has passed the Rocking Chair Test. This is something we use to guide us along the path we are taking. So when we are old and grey and sitting in our rocking chairs, we can look back on the company we

---

> created with a smile. That's why we go to the trouble of using the best quality 100% organic cotton for our shirts. The less impact our products have on the environment, the bigger the smile will be.

List any issues you have with getting going on your idea here, so you can rationalize them. Doing so will help you either remove them as obstacles, or keep them as legitimate concerns you can get around or that will ultimately prevent you from following your dreams at present.

Issues or concerns	Notes
Yours:	

Issues or concerns	Notes
Jane's:	
I had agreed to contribute towards my brother's school fees since Dad had to come away from work. It's a promise I don't want to break but it was based on my salary and bonuses.	I will need to speak to a couple of relatives that may be prepared to stand in if I can't honour this. I have this year's contribution already so I have a head start.
I was thinking of getting married and starting a family but if I decided to set up a business it would be a long time before we could think about this.	I have chatted to my partner and he agrees we can give the business a try before the baby idea and then decide.

INSIDER TIP

Just in case you think that veteran entrepreneurs don't have self doubt or issues – forget it.

Everyone does and it's right to think long and hard about your life choices.

Make sure you don't make the wrong decision, either way, it's your life and you may only get one (life that is)!

Did this exercise help you dispel any fears or doubts? I hope so. Let move on to the penultimate session now and make sure we have the support of our family and friends so that our eventual success is shared with those we love.

Mentor Session 7

Make Sure you Take your Loved Ones with You

- Achieving a life of balance
- Your family and friends
- Your circle of influence

This is a relatively short session before we take stock of everything we learnt so far in your final session. You now have all the facts about whether you should choose the life of an entrepreneur. I want you to give some thinking time to the importance of *balance* in your life, and the impact of your success as an entrepreneur on family and friends.

Remember, it's no good being the richest person in the graveyard – far too many entrepreneurs find themselves rich but totally unhappy. They sacrificed everything to get to the 'top' and when they get there they say, 'is this all there is?'. Their health, family and friends may all be the worse for wear, and they may have lost those in achieving their own definition of success.

Don't let that happen to you, by considering these issues before you start out.

Achieving a life of balance

Life is not all about work of course, even for those of us who love it and are passionate about it! Without your loved ones, why would you be doing this? You need someone to share your success with, don't you?

The big danger is to become so absorbed in your business that you lose the most important things in life like your partner, your kids and your family and friends – you will need to work really hard to balance their needs with yours in order that you can all celebrate your success as a happy and fulfilled unit.

INSIDER TIP

As if the divorce rate of about 50% (that's the national average) isn't bad enough, the rate among entrepreneurs tends to be even higher.

In my opinion, this is directly attributable to the amount of time and energy we tend to put into our businesses instead of into our families.

Watch out! It's an easy trap to fall into. Just remember that as much as you love your business, it will never love you as your partner and kids do.

They have needs, too, and you've got to be attentive to them.

Getting the balance right at home

Business ownership and a healthy personal life are both enhanced when you constantly remember that others have a stake in your success, and when *you are in control* of how your business will affect your personal life.

The easiest way to guarantee a balanced life is to build it in at the beginning of your venture. If you have a partner then consider their feelings, then make a suitable agreement that will work for everyone and stick to it.

I would strongly advise a new entrepreneur to make strict family time, and not shut his family out by not telling them what is going on (although you may wish to keep the gory details to a minimum and focus on the positive) – and just generally try to manage your time carefully.

I personally find this quite hard as I have a very busy schedule, but I have learned several great things that really help both the relationship and family time.

First, have a weekly date with your partner that can't be moved – try and get out for dinner, or a movie, or something else away from distractions and the business. Accept that this time is totally about your relationship, so leave the phone off! I often hear partners referring to new businesses as the equivalent of a 'mistress' (or toy boy!) – just think about that for a second and it will help you understand how your focus on your venture can affect others.

Apply the same idea with your kids. I try and read a bedtime story, have breakfast, or grab some times during the week when I have 30 minutes free to focus on them. Of course the weekends offer more opportunity, but again you do need to carve out some time when you are not distracted or working.

With both your kids and partner, also try and create some 'mental space' that is sacrosanct – quality time when you have a total focus on them – this means switching off from your work and clearing your mind to be free to give them total attention.

Also, think about the situation from your family's point of view. They may want to be supportive, but they do not feel your passion or see your vision. The family may only see the sacrifices they may have to make, the time you will no longer have for them, and the perceived financial risk you are taking.

Another thing people often forget is that your intimate relationship is the place of *maximum pleasure and also pain* – if your relationship is not working, then it will affect your ability to function as an entrepreneur. You must try and make both your work and play time work together. This way you will optimize your success!

Remember, it is a mistake to let the business control you. The reason many people start businesses in the first place is to get control of *their* lives. If you let your business dictate the tempo of your life, you are still no better off than working for someone else.

And by the way, try and have an external interest; "all work and no play makes jack a dull boy".

Your friends and family

Your parents and friends will want you to succeed, there's no doubt about that. However, to them, success won't always mean taking the risk of starting a business. What it really means is getting good grades, going to a great school, getting a job, and then working your way up the proverbial ladder of success. Your family may think of entrepreneurship as a distraction and discourage you from attempting it.

Your friends may wonder why you're not hanging out with them as much, and drop you from their circle.

Without the support of your friends and family, it will be that much easier for you to throw in the towel if the going gets tough. So don't alienate them – get them on your side. It could be good practice, considering all the other people you will need to win over on the road to success!

INSIDER TIP

Many of my friends are still friends but I remember having to make a brand new set when I started out as my older ones didn't really get what I was doing and we lead totally different lives.

I made the effort to find people to talk to about my business life as well as keeping in with my original friends. This has helped me keep my feet on the ground and provided me with two support networks which have often been very important to me over the years.

You may want to do the same.

Your circle of influence

As a 'pre-entrepreneurial' you may have also have a bunch of friends who would prefer you didn't change and go off to climb the mountain of your dreams, leaving them behind.

One thing you will have to face up to early on is that your friends do matter, but not perhaps your older ones. You will be turning your life on its head and you will need all the support you can get. This means avoiding negative influences and maximizing the number of positive ones. I have found my true friends accept me for what I am and support me no matter what.

> *'Who we spend time with is who we become.'*
> **Anthony Robbins**

To help you maintain the right influences from your nearest and dearest:

- Remove, avoid, or limit negative or counter-productive influences from your life.
- Don't discuss business with people who don't care or don't want to understand.
- Surround yourself with people you admire and who motivate you.
- Read about other entrepreneurs who excite you.
- Accept the fact that you're different.

It's good practice to try and find immediate peers or other business owners whom you can befriend. This advice cannot be stressed enough. I'm not advocating that you ditch all your friends, but just that you try to be very aware of the influences around you and do your best to fix or get rid of anything that's negative or counterproductive to your endeavours. You've worked very hard to get where you are. Don't let anything or anyone chip away at your success or pride in it.

INSIDER TIP

By the same token that I tried to find friends that I could relate to I also made sure I didn't waste any time with those that tried to bring me down or were negative.

It's critical that you spend time with positive and encouraging people as well as those that you respect and can learn from if you want to get a shortcut to success.

We are now on the home straight, so let's not wait. Let's move right into the final session and take stock of what we have learned.

Mentor Session 8

Are You Ready to be an Entrepreneur?

Welcome to our last mentoring session together. Each and every session has brought you closer to answering the ultimate question, **'Do you want to become an entrepreneur?'** Your learning has covered a vast amount about life as an entrepreneur and has hopefully enabled you to truly take stock of your personality, your personal resources, your motivations, your goals and your general lifestyle and how these could align with a business idea.

If you spent the time really examining what motivates and excites you in life – your passions – and then compared this to your lifestyle needs and then your business idea, you will have a much greater chance of success. My advice is to ensure that your personal goals and needs are matched to those of your business in order that you still have the passion for your endeavours many years down the road. Don't make the mistake I have made many times over of just choosing a great idea and finding out later it doesn't light my fire any more.

Business is not that difficult in reality if you are totally on 'purpose' and passionate about what you are doing, then many of the challenges will be easier and you will able to maintain your momentum for the long term – and this is critical to the success of your venture. By now you will know if you are willing to do whatever it takes to get a business off the ground and running successfully.

Does your dream and business idea match your personal needs and ambitions? Did you start out with an idea and have you now matched that, or rejected it based on what you have learned? Maybe you have tweaked it a little so that it is now focused on <u>providing you with the life you deserve</u>.

Have you thought about your personality, resources and skills, and thought about whether your role in the business matches what you are best at and will give you the greatest fulfilment? Did you learn that you have great assets and characteristics that apply to being an entrepreneur, and also weaknesses for which you can find team members to complement your abilities?

If you started out with no idea about what you could do, then you have probably come up with a list of potential business ideas based on your learnings from this book. They should stem from the things you love and are passionate about, jobs you would do even if you didn't get paid. Of course, maybe it became clear you just needed a new job in another field or with another employer. An equally valid finding.

If you do have an idea and are itching to get started, step back and ask yourself a few final questions to check if you have chosen the right path:

- Does your business idea sound like it will still excite you and make you want to leap out of bed in two years' time?
- Are you sure it matches your lifestyle needs and enables you to do what you love, even in the future?
- Have you thought out the impact on your relationships and considered who you want to work with yet?

So what are your answers to the ultimate question – do you want to be entrepreneur?

At the beginning of our journey together I asked you to consider a set of ten questions. These quick questions were designed to help you come to an ultimate conclusion about whether or not you want to become an entrepreneur. I encouraged you to take notes along the way, to clarify your thinking or raise any points of concern. You should now have a clear answer to all of them. If you don't, please spend time and go back through the Mentoring Sessions making notes until you are clear.

As you know, your fellow mentee, Jane, has been diligently following the same set of exercises with you. Jane is going to share her revised set of answers with me and I will attempt to give her some further guidance and agree some next steps. Please use this as an opportunity to examine your own answers in deciding if you do want to become an entrepreneur. Download the form (www .tobeanentrepreneur.com) and complete it by going back through your answers in each of the sessions.

Top ten ways to answer the ultimate question – do I want to become an entrepreneur?

Name: *Jane Toomey*

---

1 What characteristics do you share with successful entrepreneurs?

Jane:
I share confidence, ability to take action, good communication skills and integrity.

Jon:
What a great start! Your initial personality quiz responses were good, so I'm not surprised. These characteristics, like the other traits we spoke about, can be learnt and those you where you were weaker can simply be exercised. Like a muscle!

2 What are your reasons for wanting to become an entrepreneur?

Jane:

I want the freedom to follow my vision in life, not someone else's. I want to have a job that isn't a million miles away from what I love to do anyway. I want to be able to decide on my hours based on how I work best.

Jon:

These are all solid reasons and being an entrepreneur will help you achieve those things. Do you feel a passion that will propel you yet?

3 How would your family and friends react to you becoming an entrepreneur?

Jane:

As long as I have done all my due diligence and I am basing the business on something that I enjoy, have experience in and have an aptitude for, then I think they will support me. I also need to make sure they are involved in the process and get excited and motivated with me. I also need to make sure I make quality time for them no matter how involved I get in the business. Basically I need to use those great communication skills of mine.

Jon:

Great, you have picked up on one of the important things. You need to demonstrate to your family and friends that you are not going into this blind. Show them all the work you have put in here for starters. Then when you do finally get started, include them and inform them but most of all make separate time for them.

4   What do you think your life would be like on a day-to-day basis?

Jane:

I think it will range from what I do now, all the logistical stuff around catering, the cooking and creative side to secretarial to banking to sales and marketing to making the tea of course. I am under no illusions.

Jon:

Have you considered what will be your core roles and skills and those you will delegate? If not, then try and think about who else will plug any skills gaps. Also, you will need to think about your routine as a new entrepreneur and consider how you will deal with the loneliness and stresses of the job; perhaps you could join a local entrepreneur group or round up any other entrepreneurs you know as support.

5   What do you think the downsides are and how would you cope with them?

Jane:

I think for me it will be being on my own a lot and making decisions on my own. There aren't any networking groups relevant to the industry I want to go into, although there are some general ones. However, I intend to start one!

Jon:

Well done, that's the spirit! Make sure you get some quality time with your partner too and ask them for support and guidance. Having them part of the 'team' will help you in the early days before you hire some people.

6 What is your vision and personal mission?

Jane:
Vision

I see my life free from the corporate shackles and working for myself. I am bringing- happiness to customers and family alike with my cooking and recipes. I am also educating people on the importance of healthy organic food that hasn't had to travel thousands of miles to get to their plate. I am changing the eating habits of a generation of kids.

My personal mission statement

'I will start my business within 3 months and plan to grow it to £500,000 in revenues within a year. Using this success my staff and I will spread the word to local schools and businesses about eco-friendly food production in order that we reach at least 100 people within the same time frame. My purpose will be to massively add value to our local community in measurable ways that have a real impact on people's health now and in the future'

Jon:
These are great, they have specific outcomes, timescales and sound motivational. They will no

doubt change over time or get more refined, but it's great that you can align your life plans with your business dream.

7   What are your core personality traits?

Jane:

I am individualistic, stubborn, attentive to others, thick-skinned, confident, self reliant, trusting tolerant, attached and impatient.

Jon:

Looks like you will make a great start-up entrepreneur but also pay attention to the needs of others and the team. You know you can be stubborn, so make a special effort work at this and take the needs of others into consideration.

8   What life stage are you at and how do you think this will affect your chances?

Jane:

I am not mortgaged yet and don't have a family, so that means I am relatively low risk. I have got some commitments but I plan to move in with my partner Mark and use some of my savings to honour my family commitments (helping to pay brother's school fees). I am young but quite experienced in my field which hopefully will impress potential investors. I am also going to take on a couple of part-time jobs at the weekend to help put some money aside. I do want to get married and start a family at some point but I will give the business 2 years and make a decision then.

Jon:

You are at a great life stage, you have experience but your cost base and responsibilities are still quite low. This makes the risk low, as you say, and also leaves plenty of opportunity to jump back on the job ladder if you need to. Also, you can start your business quite small with little cash, so no worries about the money.

9 What resources do you have available to you?

Jane:

I have a family friend already in the catering business on the equipment supply side and he has lots of great contacts as well as some cut-price equipment. I have already tentatively secured some investment from a relative — as long as he likes the business case. He has also put me in touch with some good business angels — he won't fund the whole thing! Lastly, I have made contact with some old school friends who are in marketing. They have agreed to help and one even wants to come on board!

Jon:

Wow, you really have taken full advantage of the process in the book to get yourself fully prepared. This all sounds very good.

10 What can you see yourself doing for the rest of your life?

Jane:

I see myself working around catering and cooking for the rest of my days. This is what makes me happier than anything else. I am so passionate about it, especially good healthy organic food and I want *to tell the world about it. I can hardly believe it might be possible to do it for the rest of my life . . . and make a living from it.*

Jon:
I think you have the maximum chance of success; you are so aligned between your business and your passions. This will drive you when things inevitably become tough.

OK, how did you do on the ten questions the second time around?

How do your answers look after reading the book vs. when you started? Do you have a real clarity in your thoughts now and do you have what you need to make your decision?

So what will it be – will you now go on to become an entrepreneur?

Best of luck in whatever your choice is and I am sure if you followed this book you will now be much clearer about what you want out of life like I promised at the start.

Next steps . . .
I hope that you have enjoyed this book and have made the right life decision for you. You are now armed with all you need to take the next step, and explore your idea and dreams further to decide if you can make a successful business out of them.

This is the beginning . . . now it's up to you to get started.

There are many great books to read and other useful resources as you continue your journey, and a list of these can be found on our website: www.tobeanentrepreneur.com

Epilogue

In this section we hear about the fictional Jane's experiences as a way to summarise what you have learned.

So let's hear from Jane for the last time and imagine her journey:

Jon asked me to tell you all about the journey I have taken in the last year and a half, and why I've found the mentor sessions invaluable in getting me to where I am — or where I am going, as I still have so much to achieve and learn. I can't believe I finally get to write one of these things. I remember trying to come up with my business idea and writing . . '2 years ago I started . . .' And here I am . . .

I was once sitting where you are now. I had a vague understanding of what it meant to be an entrepreneur, much of it was stuff I had gleaned from TV shows and news clips of the latest global entrepreneur launching his next great product. I had little idea of what it meant as a lifestyle choice. I didn't know if I was really suited to it or if my early ideas would be realistic, considering the type of person I am and the things that are important to me in life.

We started out by doing some very high-level personality tests, which got me thinking about who I am and what I am good at. We then examined some of the known consistent traits in entrepreneurs and I got a chance to see how I measured up against these and what things I needed to develop. After learning more about the myths and real life of entrepreneurs we got into the interesting stuff — documenting all the things I have done and the things I am good at and seeing if they could support a decision to become an entrepreneur. After recording all the people and resources I had available to me it became clear that I had what it takes — not only that, but I had a great business idea.

After I finished Jon's course I developed a business plan in my spare time, using the resources I had available to me for support and input. I also did a part-time bookkeeping and financial planning course. I then went and spoke to a business angel after already securing some initial investment from a family friend. After a couple of knock backs I finally got the green light (I did have to make some changes to my business, but it was worth it). I happily handed in my notice to the catering firm where I worked and immediately registered Jane's Jolly Green Groceries & Home Catering Business Ltd. I deliver groceries and healthy ready meals to home workers and the incapacitated, and now to small businesses. I have a team of three people, one of whom is a real whizz in systems; the other two are great sales and marketing people, and together we all really believe in wholesome, organic, home-grown food delivered to your door. Right now we all cycle the delivery bikes to the destinations, but I plan to hire a number of delivery boys and girls so I can concentrate on my next big idea. The only problem is deciding which one to go with next . . .

Answer key

Compare your answers to the Quiz with the answer key that follows choosing the best result. Give yourself 2 points for those that match the key and 0 points for the rest.

X is most or least like the statement below	Answers	X	Score
In most things *x* does, s/he will keep going until it is completed.	M		
When *x* has set his/her mind on something, s/he continues even when there are obstacles.	M		
Once *x* sets an objective, s/he works towards it until the end of the day and then leaves for another time if not complete.	L		
x is always full of new ideas and dreams.	M		
x is rather afraid of standing out from the crowd or sticking her/his neck out.	L		
x is a creature of habit and likes to do things in the same way that s/he is used to.	L		
x can be very single-minded and will then shut out all other needs and influences.	M		
When *x* pursues a sport or hobby s/he gives up if s/he doesn't do well the first few times at it.	L		

People readily confide in x and seek him/her out for advice or a sympathetic ear.	**M**		
x is not very good at deceiving and cheating and it bothers her/him for a long time afterwards when s/he does.	**M**		
x is open and enthusiastic about her/his ideas and opinions and shares them readily with other people.	**M**		
If x believes in something, s/he is easily knocked off course by the opinions of others.	**L**		
x tends to do things right the first time, s/he doesn't change his/her approach.	**L**		
Although s/he can be a dreamer at times, most of every day x is active and on the go.	**M**		
x seems to operate on the assumption that it is better to have tried and failed than never to have tried at all.	**M**		
x will often attempt to solve problems or fix things even though s/he does not have the skills for it.	**M**		
x frequently has to be spurred on and encouraged by me and others.	**L**		
x is happy to live his/her life without uncertainty and don't like making leaps of faith	**L**		
Before x makes an important decision, s/he usually asks for feedback from people s/he respects.	**M**		
If x had to choose between paying herself/himself and a staff member, s/he will pay herself/himself first	**L**		

✗ is methodical and strategic and usually has a plan of action before starting a project.	M		
✗ is suspicious that others may steal or appropriate his/her ideas.	L		
✗ usually finds it hard to stand up and talk to an audience.	L		
✗ seems to feel that s/he deserves the good things in life.	M		
On the whole people seem to understand ✗ clearly and easily.	M		
✗ learns more readily by doing rather than studying and reflecting.	M		
✗ acts based on clear evidence and doesn't like to make decisions otherwise even if s/he has no choice	L		
Beyond having a vague image, ✗ is able to visualize future scenarios in quite some detail.	M		
✗ tends to honor her/his commitments and promises, even if it puts her/him out.	M		
✗ resorts to white lies occasionally in order to beat the competition.	L		
After making a decision, ✗ sometimes wonders whether s/he made the right one.	L		
In order to get a good deal, ✗ is likely to be economical with the truth.	L		
✗ gets easily frustrated if s/he doesn't receive immediate rewards for her/his efforts.	L		
✗ can get easily rattled by others and feels undermined or insecure when others disagree.	L		

Faced with a sudden change in plans, x can usually come up with several alternatives quickly.	**M**		
x seems to have an innate faith in life, that s/he will always land on her/his feet.	**M**		
x can get drawn into the detail of problems, losing the bigger picture.	**L**		
x is willing to take risks and bear the consequences.	**M**		
x can't openly challenge people and speak her/his mind.	**L**		
x is known to have made intuitive decisions, without much rational evidence, and on the whole they have worked out.	**M**		
x always looks for new ways of doing things and is a keen learner.	**M**		
x may make mistakes, but s/he does not get into thinking of herself/ himself as a bad, deficient, incapable person.	**M**		
x tends to be focused on today rather than a long term dream.	**L**		
x will sometimes miss a meal in order to finish what s/he are doing.	**M**		
x frequently questions received wisdom and ignores advice from authorities, preferring to do her/his own thing or find out for herself/ himself.	**M**		
x tends to put her/his hobbies first and does not allow work interfere with them.	**L**		
x easily gets worried about money and financial security.	**L**		

After x has an idea s/he likes to think long and hard about it before getting it started	L		
When things go wrong for x or s/he experiences setbacks, it tends to spur her/him on and make her/him more determined.	M		
x is not keen on surprises, and gets irritated when s/he has to change her/his plans.	L		
On the whole people seem to understand x clearly and easily.	L		
TOTAL MATCHES – adding up all the scores for a total			

Mark all the answers you got a match for and add 2 points, zero for the rest. Write the total out of 100. This gives you the percentage of answers that are the best fit to the ideal profile. This gives you your EQ (Entrepreneurial Quotient).

My EQ (Entrepreneurial Quotient)	%

The higher the percentage, the greater the possibility that you are suited to be an entrepreneur and the closer you are to exhibiting the characteristics of successful entrepreneurs.

Index